A WORLD BANK STUDY

Early Child Education

Making Programs Work for Brazil's Most Important Generation

David K. Evans
Katrina Kosec

THE WORLD BANK
Washington, D.C.

© 2012 International Bank for Reconstruction and Development / The World Bank
1818 H Street NW, Washington DC 20433
Telephone: 202-473-1000; Internet: www.worldbank.org

Some rights reserved

1 2 3 4   15 14 13 12

World Bank Studies are published to communicate the results of the Bank's work to the development community with the least possible delay. The manuscript of this paper therefore has not been prepared in accordance with the procedures appropriate to formally edited texts.

This work is a product of the staff of The World Bank with external contributions. Note that The World Bank does not necessarily own each component of the content included in the work. The World Bank therefore does not warrant that the use of the content contained in the work will not infringe on the rights of third parties. The risk of claims resulting from such infringement rests solely with you.

The findings, interpretations, and conclusions expressed in this work do not necessarily reflect the views of The World Bank, its Board of Executive Directors, or the governments they represent. The World Bank does not guarantee the accuracy of the data included in this work. The boundaries, colors, denominations, and other information shown on any map in this work do not imply any judgment on the part of The World Bank concerning the legal status of any territory or the endorsement or acceptance of such boundaries.

Nothing herein shall constitute or be considered to be a limitation upon or waiver of the privileges and immunities of The World Bank, all of which are specifically reserved.

Rights and Permissions

This work is available under the Creative Commons Attribution 3.0 Unported license (CC BY 3.0) http://creativecommons.org/licenses/by/3.0. Under the Creative Commons Attribution license, you are free to copy, distribute, transmit, and adapt this work, including for commercial purposes, under the following conditions:

Attribution—Please cite the work as follows: Evans, David K. and Katrina Kosec. 2012. *Early Child Education: Making Programs Work for Brazil's Most Important Generation*. Washington, D.C.: World Bank. DOI: 10.1596/978-0-8213-8931-7 License: Creative Commons Attribution CC BY 3.0

Translations—If you create a translation of this work, please add the following disclaimer along with the attribution: *This translation was not created by The World Bank and should not be considered an official World Bank translation. The World Bank shall not be liable for any content or error in this translation.*

All queries on rights and licenses should be addressed to the Office of the Publisher, The World Bank, 1818 H Street NW, Washington, DC 20433, USA; fax: 202-522-2625; e-mail: pubrights@worldbank.org.

ISBN (paper): 978-0-8213-8931-7
ISBN (electronic): 978-0-8213-9563-9
DOI: 10.1596/978-0-8213-8931-7

Cover photo: Courtesy of Barbara Bruns. The girls in this photo were attending a creche (daycare center) in Rio de Janeiro, Brazil.

Library of Congress Cataloging-in-Publication Data has been requested.

Contents

Acknowledgments vii
Acronyms and Abbreviations ix
Executive Summary xi

1. **Early Child Education—A Top Priority for the Coming Years** 1
   Why Are Early Child Development and Early Child Education So Important? 1
   How Has Brazil Advanced in Early Child Development and Early Child
      Education in Recent Years? 7
   Key Issues Facing Brazil in Early Child Education 11

2. **Ensuring High Quality Early Child Education for Brazil's Children** 14
   Current Quality of Early Child Education in Brazil 14
   Curricular and Program Structure Improvement 25
   Monitoring Program Quality 25
   Improving Quality through Improved Incentives 28
   Improving Quality through Improved In-Service Training and Supervision 29
   Improving Quality through Knowledge Sharing 29
   Lessons 31

3. **How to Reach the Very Poorest Children** 33
   Access to Early Child Education around the World 33
   How Has Access to Early Child Education Evolved in Brazil? 34
   Reaching the Poorest: How Many to Plan For 44
   Building New Centers 47
   Alternative Ways to Deliver Early Child Education 50
   Provision and Financing of Early Child Education 52
   Lessons 57

4. **The Next Steps for Brazil's Children** 59
   Cross-Sectoral Collaboration 59
   Leveraging Private Sector Provision, Funding, and Innovation 64
   Compensating for Differences across Municipalities 66
   Lessons 69

Appendixes 71
   Appendix A: Pre-school Enrollment with Alternative Definitions 73
   Appendix B: Survey of Evidence for Early Child Education in Brazil 74
   Appendix C: Rio de Janeiro's Creche Lottery 75
   Appendix D: Quality Rating Systems 76

Appendix E: Selected Child Development Instruments 77
Appendix F: Curriculum for Primeira Infância Completa 78
Appendix G: Selection of MEC Publications for Early Childhood Development ... 79
Appendix H: Jamaica's National Strategic Plan for Early Childhood
Development 80

References 81

Boxes

Box 2.1: Impact evaluation for early child development 28
Box 2.2: Training and supervision in two municipalities 29

Figures

Figure 1: ECE coverage by state, 2009 xii
Figure 2: ECE access by income quintile xiii
Figure 3: Quality of creches and pre-schools in six capital municipalities xiv
Figure 4: Additional children enrolled following revenue shock that leads median
municipality to enroll 100 more children xv
Figure 5: Fraction of creche students in public vs. private institutions by quintile
of income (2009) xvii
Figure 6: Fraction of pre-school students in public vs. private institutions by
quintile of income (2009) xvii
Figure 1.1: Cognitive development across income differentials over time 2
Figure 1.2: Impact of high-quality, highly targeted early child education programs 4
Figure 1.3: Sample of large-scale programs 7
Figure 1.4: Public child investments per capita, 2006–2009 10
Figure 1.5: Fraction of children enrolled in early child education (1996–2009) 12
Figure 2.1: Average quality index of creches and pre-schools by region (2001 and
2009) 16
Figure 2.2: Average number of students per classroom, by year and region 17
Figure 2.3: Average infrastructure quality index of creches and pre-schools in
Brazil by administrative dependency (2009) 17
Figure 2.4: Distribution of creche quality by broad quality domain 19
Figure 2.5: Distribution of creche quality by selected specific areas 19
Figure 2.6: Distribution of quality across ECE institutions 20
Figure 2.7: Level of education of teachers in ECE versus primary and lower-
secondary school 21
Figure 2.8: Fraction of teachers with higher (post-secondary) education, by year
and region 22
Figure 2.9: Relationship between observed creche quality and parents' subjective
measure of quality, Rio de Janeiro, 2001 24
Figure 3.1: Creche enrollment around the world, age 0–3 (or as specified) 33
Figure 3.2: Pre-school enrollment around the world 34
Figure 3.3: Fraction of 0–3 children in creche, 1996–2009 35
Figure 3.4: Fraction of 4–6 children in pre-school, 1996–2009 35

Figure 3.5: Creche access by state, 2009 36
Figure 3.6: Pre-school access by state, 2009 36
Figure 3.7: Fraction of 0–3 children in creche by gender (1996–2009) 37
Figure 3.8: Fraction of 4–6 children in pre-school by gender (1996–2009) 38
Figure 3.9: ECE institution attendance by income (1996–2009) 38
Figure 3.10: Fraction of children enrolled in creche in public vs. private institutions by income quintile (2009) 39
Figure 3.11: Fraction of children attending pre-school in public vs. private institutions by income quintile (2009) 40
Figure 3.12: Fraction of 4–6 children in pre-school by rural/urban, 1996–2009 41
Figure 3.13: Fraction of 4–6 children in pre-school by income and rural/urban, 1996–2009 41
Figure 3.14: Creche enrollment by mother's work status, 1996–2009 43
Figure 3.15: Pre-school enrollment by mother's work status, 1996–2009 43
Figure 3.16: Creche participation in Rio de Janeiro, by income level 46
Figure 3.17: Number of public creches by region, 2001–2009 47
Figure 3.18: Share of creches of different administrative dependencies, by region 52
Figure 3.19: Share of pre-schools of different administrative dependencies, by region 53
Figure 3.20: Fraction of early child education students in unregistered institutions, by year and region 54
Figure 4.1: Additional children enrolled following revenue shock that leads median municipality to enroll 100 more children 67
Figure C.1: Lottery process for municipality of Rio de Janeiro, 2007–2010 75

Tables

Table 1: Sample of evidence on impacts of early child education in Brazil xi
Table 1.1: Sample of Brazilian evidence on impacts of early child education 4
Table 1.2: Policy changes in early child education in Brazil 8
Table 1.3: Starting age for compulsory education in Europe, North America, and selected other countries 8
Table 1.4: Child health outcomes across the world in 2007 10
Table 2.1: Impact of creche quality on months of child development, measured in months of child development 15
Table 2.2: Domains in early child education observation instruments 18
Table 2.3: Teacher qualifications required in Brazil and comparator countries 23
Table 3.1: Labor force participation across countries 42
Table 3.2: Total number of children not enrolled in ECE, by region 44
Table 3.3: Number of 4–5 year olds not enrolled in pre-school in 2009, by rural/urban and region 45
Table 3.4: Estimated demand for creche, by region 46
Table 3.5: Average enrollment size of pre-schools in 2009, by region 47
Table 3.6: ECE institutions, by type of institution (2005, 2009) 49
Table 3.7: Method for identifying locations for new ECE centers 50

Table 3.8: Annual municipal early child education expenditures in 2009, by region 55
Table 4.1: Brazil's National Plan for Early Childhood 61
Table 4.2: Services offered under Chile Crece Contigo 63
Table 4.3: Steps to establishing public-private partnerships for ECD 66
Table A.1: ECE enrollment rate by year and definition of enrollment 73
Table B.1: Survey of studies of impact of ECE in Brazil 74
Table D.1: Quality standards used to rate ECD centers 76
Table D.2: Rating systems for early child development centers 76
Table E.1: Sample of child assessment instruments used in creches and pre-schools 77
Table F.1: Curriculum implemented as of November 2009 78
Table G.1: Selection of MEC publications for ECE 79
Table H.1: Jamaica's National Strategic Plan for Early Childhood Development 80

Acknowledgments

This report draws deeply on the extraordinary efforts and innovations demonstrated by early child development policy makers around Brazil. Many of these policy makers have given generously of their time and shared information about programs highlighted in this report, including Maria do Pilar Lacerda Almeida, former Secretary of Basic Education; Rita Coelho, Early Child Education coordinator at the Ministry of Education; Claudia Costin, Secretary of Education for the Municipality of Rio de Janeiro; Maria Correa, former Secretary of Education for the State of Acre; Osmar Terra, former Secretary of Health for the State of Rio Grande do Sul; Célia Gedeon, Elaine Pazello, and Gabriela Moriconi at the National Education Research Institute (INEP); Ricardo Paes de Barros, Secretary of the Office of Strategic Action in the Secretariat for Strategic Affairs of the Presidency of Brazil; and Mirela de Carvalho at the Rio de Janeiro State Secretariat of Education.

This report draws on background papers about innovations in early child education in Rio de Janeiro and in caregiver training and supervision in two municipalities within São Paulo state. The authors of the Rio de Janeiro study are Ricardo Paes de Barros, Mirela de Carvalho, Samuel Franco, Eduardo de Pádua, and Andrezza Rosalém. The authors of the São Paulo studies are Joseane Bomfim, Marisa Vasconcelos Ferreira, and Zilma de Moraes Ramos de Oliveira. The report also draws on a host of early child education research from around Brazil: Maria Malta Campos of Fundação Carlos Chagas, Aimee Verdisco of the Inter-American Development Bank, and Fabiana Felicio all contributed with valuable information on their research.

Peer reviewers at both the beginning and completion of the project provided valuable feedback, specifically Harold Alderman, Felipe Barrera, João Batista Oliveira, Maria Thereza Marcilio, Robert Myers, Sophie Naudeau, Daniel Santos, and Mary Eming Young. Steven Barnett of Rutgers University supplied helpful feedback at various points. The Maria Cecilia Souto Vidigal Foundation provided excellent comments and supported the publication of the Portuguese edition of this report: "Educação Infantil: Programas para a Geração Mais Importante do Brasil." Colleagues at the World Bank contributed with readings of the draft and strategic suggestions, including Erica Amorim, Laura Chioda, Tito Cordella, Margaret Grosh, and Emiliana Vegas. In particular, Madalena dos Santos, Michele Gragnolati, Chingboon Lee, and Barbara Bruns provided detailed, crucial inputs. The World Bank Brazil administrative staff—Mariane Brito, Marize Santos, and Carla Zardo—facilitated countless meetings and communications with Brazilian policy makers.

The report has especially benefitted from the support and encouragement of the World Bank country director for Brazil, Deborah Wetzel, and the former World Bank country director for Brazil, Makhtar Diop.

The team accepts full responsibility for any errors.

Acronyms and Abbreviations

Asinhas	*Asas da Florestania Infantil*/Children's Wings of Florestania
ChCC	*Chile Crece Contigo*/Chile Grows With You
CLASS	Classroom Assessment Scoring System
CNPq	National Council for Scientific and Technological Development
CONAFE	*Consejo Nacional de Fomento Educativo*
ECD	Early Child Development
ECE	Early Child Education
ECERS-R	Early Childhood Environment Rating Scale—Revised for pre-schools
EDIs	*Espaços de desenvolvimento infantil*/Early Child Development Spaces
Educa a Su Hijo	Educate Your Child
ERSs	Environmental Rating Scales
ESAC	*Escala de Avaliação de Ambientes para Bebês e Crianças Pequenas/ Escala de Avaliação de Ambientes da Educação Infantil*
EU	European Union
FLFP	Female Labor Force Participation
FPE/ FPM	State and Municipal Participation Funds
FPG	Child Development Institute
FUNDEB	Fund for the Maintenance and Development of Basic Education
FUNDEF	Fund for the Maintenance and Development of Elementary Education and Teacher Development
GDP	Gross Domestic Product
IADB	Inter-American Development Bank
IBGE	*Instituto Brasileiro de Geografia e Estatística*/Brazilian Institute of Geography and Statistics
ICMS	*Imposto sobre Operações relativas à Circulação de Mercadorias e Prestação de Serviços de Transporte Interestadual e Intermunicipal e de Comunicação* (state tax on goods and services)
INEP	*Instituto Nacional de Estudos e Pesquisas Educacionais Anisio Teixeira*
IPEA	Institute for Applied Economic Research
IPIexp	The export-proportional excise tax
IPVA	The motor vehicles tax
IRmuni and IRest	Income tax benefits levied on income paid by the municipalities or the state
ITCMD	The tax on inheritance and donations
ITERS-R	Infant and Toddler Environment Rating Scale—Revised for creches
ITR	The 50% share of the rural territory tax due to municipalities
LC 87/96	Transfers under the complementary law

LDB	Law of Directives and Bases of National Education
LFP	Labor force participation
MEC	Ministry of Education
MINEDUC	*Ministerio de Educación*
NACCRRA	National Association of Child Care Resource & Referral Agencies
NAEHCY	National Association for the Education of Homeless Children and Youth
NGA	National Governor's Assocation
NSP	National Strategic Plan for Early Childhood Development
OECD	Organization for Economic Co-operation and Development
PB	Participatory budgeting
PIM	*Primeira Infância Melhor*/Better Early Childhood
PNAD	*Pesquisa Nacional por Amostra de Domicilios*
QRS	Quality Rating Systems
Rede Nacional Primeira Infância	National Network for Early Childhood
SEE	State Education Secretariat
UNDIME	The National Union of Municipal Education Leaders
UNESCO	United Nations Educational, Scientific, and Cultural Organization
UNICEF	United Nations Children's Fund
WB	World Bank
WHO	World Health Organization

Exchange Rate Effective May 28, 2011

Currency Unit	=	Brazil Real (BRL)
BRL$1.00	=	US$0.63
US$1.00	=	BRL$1.59

Executive Summary

The Facts

Early child education (ECE) can have lasting positive impacts on children, with benefits far exceeding the costs. But quality is crucial. Evidence from the United States, Argentina, Chile, and elsewhere has shown long-term positive impacts of early child education. That evidence is now complemented by data from Brazil showing positive impacts of early child education—particularly pre-school—on short-run cognitive development, medium-run test scores, and long-run educational attainment and income (table 1). But simply enrolling children in ECE is no guarantee of success. Evidence from Brazil shows that children who attend low-quality pre-schools perform the same on literacy tests two years later as do children who attend no pre-school at all, whereas children in high-quality pre-schools perform much better. Good ECE centers are characterized by quality in a range of areas: safe and appropriate infrastructure, effective daily program structures, personal care routines, interactions with staff, and activities to promote physical, social, and cognitive development.

Table 1: Sample of evidence on impacts of early child education in Brazil

Sample	Results
Southeast & Northeast	Almost half an additional year of schooling by adulthood Two to six percent increase in future earnings for men (more for those coming from illiterate households)
Campo Grande, Florianópolis, Teresina	Positive significant impact on *Provinha Brasil* (second grade literacy) results, particularly for children who attended high-quality pre-schools
Sertãozinho	*Provinha Brasil* results six percent higher for children with ECE
Rio de Janeiro	Positive impacts of high-quality creche participation on mental and social development while still in creche
Nationally representative	Positive impact of creche participation on fourth-grade math scores

Source: World Bank.

ECE matters most for the poorest children. ECE is likely to have the greatest positive impacts on children from poorer and less-educated families where there is less cognitive stimulation at home. In Ecuador and in the United States, poor children have been shown to start out cognitively disadvantaged due to less stimulation at home, and to grow more disadvantaged over time. Poor children need these programs the most and see the highest returns from them. In Brazil, a study of adults in the Northeast and Southeast regions demonstrated that pre-school had bigger impacts on children with illiterate parents than on children with literate parents. Internationally, the strongest evidence for the value of ECE comes from high-quality programs closely targeting the most vulnerable children.

Pro-child government policies have laid the groundwork for past and future advances in ECE. The last 20 years of early child policy in Brazil have significantly improved the situation for children and paved the way for future improvements. The Federal Constitution of 1988 made children citizens and added ECE to the purview of the Ministry of Education, underscoring the educational as well as the social welfare-based motivation for ECE. The starting age in Brazil for formal education has been decreasing over time, from seven prior to 1996 to six in 2007, and finally—by constitutional amendment—to four in 2009. Brazil's school starting age is now among the youngest in the world. Two school finance laws have also helped partially equalize access to education financing. First, in 1998, FUNDEF provided more education funds to municipalities— particularly those in the poorest states—potentially freeing up funds for ECE. In 2007, FUNDEB specifically paid municipalities for enrolling children in ECE. Both laws have helped make an early school starting age a real possibility for Brazil's children.

There are stark disparities in ECE coverage across states, with some requiring massive expansions in the coming years to achieve intended universal pre-school coverage by 2016. Achieving universal enrollment in pre-school for children ages 4–5 will require almost 1.6 million new spaces. Expanding creche enrollment to even thirty percent of children would require over 1.3 million new spaces. Behind these massive numbers lies great variation across states (figure 1). Six states have pre-school enrollment rates under 60 percent, meaning that universal coverage would require almost doubling enrollment over five years. Likewise, six states have creche enrollment rates under 10 percent, requiring massive expansion to reach the most vulnerable children.

Poor children and rural children are being left behind in early child education. Brazil's poorest children are by far the least likely to be enrolled in creche or pre-school, and those poor children that are enrolled are much more likely to rely on public schools than are their richer peers. The richest children are three times as likely to be in creche as the poorest children and 24 percent more likely to be in pre-school (figure 2). This difference exacerbates disparities in opportunity that—without intervention—will follow these children throughout their education. Not only are wealthier families much more

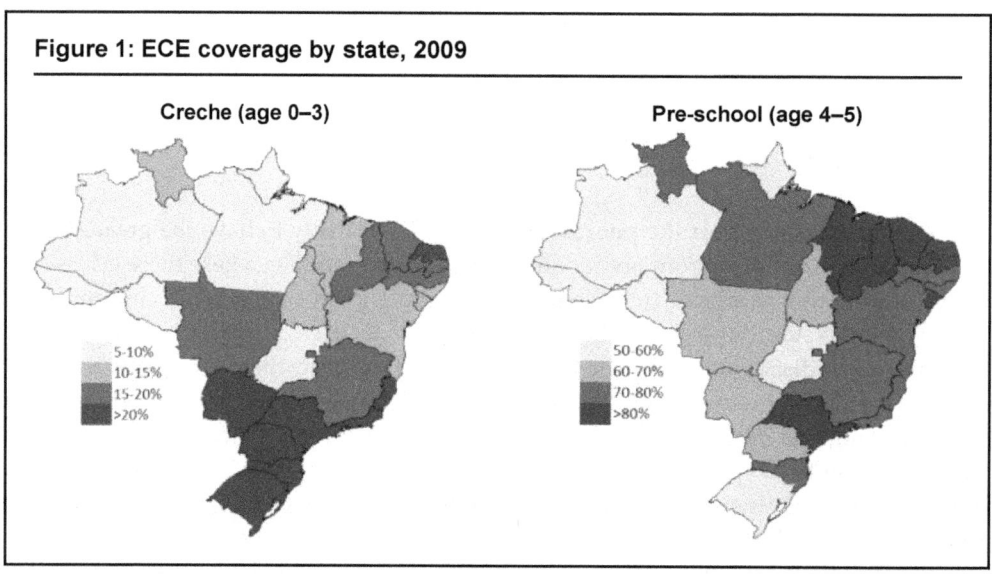

Source: Data from PNAD (2009).
Note: Creche access is the enrollment rate in schools for children aged 0–3. Pre-school access is the enrollment rate in schools for children aged 4–5.

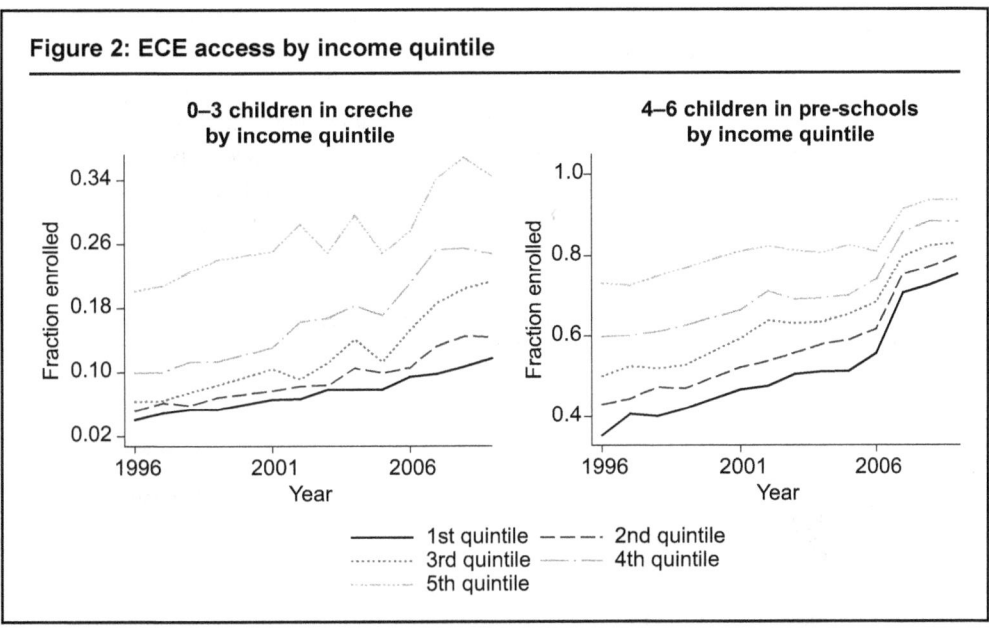

Source: Pesquisa Nacional por Amostra de Domicilios (PNAD), 1996-2009.
Note: Before 2007, the pre-school attendance rate is the fraction of 4–6 year olds in pre-school. Beginning in 2007, the pre-school attendance rate is the fraction of 4–6 year olds in institutions intended for 4–6 year olds.

likely to provide their children with early child education: they are much more likely to use the private system. More than 85 percent of the poorest children who are in ECE use public institutions, compared with only about 20 percent of the wealthiest children. Because private institutions tend to be of higher quality (at least in terms of infrastructure and teacher training), this gap further intensifies inequality of opportunity.

Rural households are much poorer than urban households, so it is unsurprising that rural children have lower enrollment in ECE. However, the poorest urban children participate in pre-school at the same rate as the wealthiest rural children, so income does not capture the full rural-urban disparity. Rural children have less access to early child education, likely because low population density makes center-based care much more expensive in rural areas.

Quality in ECE centers in Brazil has improved over time but is still weak, particularly in activities to stimulate cognitive development. In certain key indicators, such as physical infrastructure and caregiver-child ratios, ECE centers have improved over the past decade. Creches across the country have become more likely to have a dedicated school building, an indoor bathroom, electricity, a library, a computer, and connections to public sewer networks. Pre-schools likewise have improved across an array of infrastructure measures. Good infrastructure is an essential but far from sufficient condition for a high-quality ECE experience. Attention to children is also essential. Creches in Brazil maintained a constant child-caregiver ratio of 26 over the last decade, while pre-schools improved from 39 to 32. However, this compares unfavorably with the recommendations from the United States' National Association for the Education of Young Children that even five-year-olds have a maximum of ten children per caregiver, and that younger children have much lower ratios. A recent study of creches and pre-schools in six capital municipalities around Brazil found that ECE centers were strongest on interactions between caregivers and children, and weakest on activities and a consistent program structure that lends itself to cognitive, social, and emotional development. Specifically, ECE centers lacked a program structure with a schedule, free play, group time, provisions for disabled children, and activities such as block play, musical and movement activities, and science activities. Overall, using a scale that has been applied in several countries, 50 percent of creches and 30 percent of pre-schools rated inadequate, and none rated excellent (figure 3). Quality outside capital municipalities is likely to be even lower.

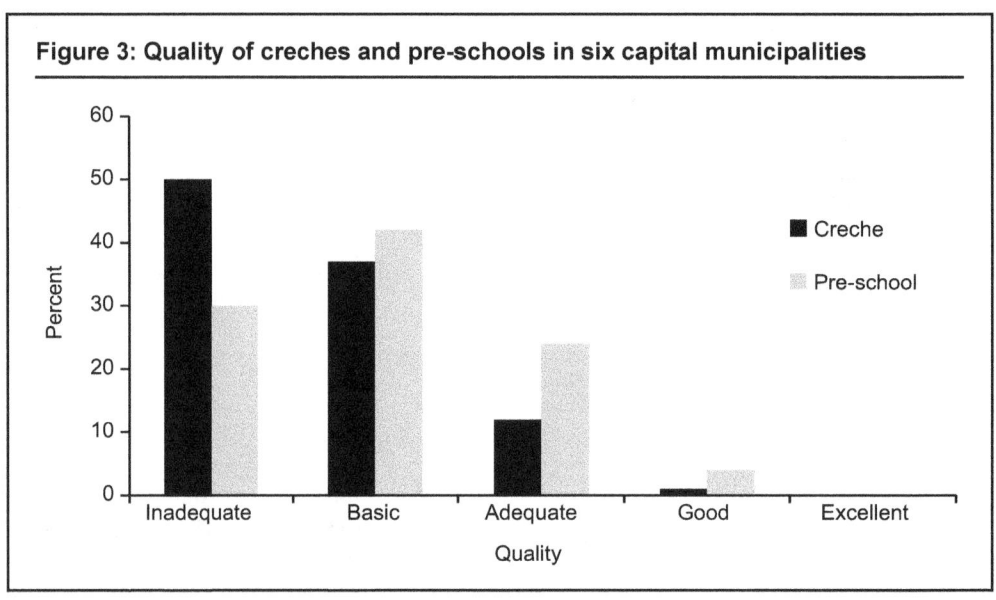

Source: Fundação Carlos Chagas (2010).

The quality of ECE centers varies dramatically across regions by infrastructure, teacher quality, and activities, as does spending per pupil. On an index of infrastructure quality, pre-schools in the Southeast had twice the infrastructure quality of pre-schools in the North (and creches were almost as disparate). Concretely, all pre-schools in the South and Southeast had electricity in 2009, whereas only three-quarters of pre-schools in the North did. Creches in the North had 70 percent more students per classroom than did creches in the South, clearly affecting students' experience at an age when caregiver-child interaction is very important. Private creches also greatly surpass public centers in infrastructure quality. Not only do the North and Northeast need expansions in coverage; they also need substantive quality improvements (as do even the highest quality regions, the South and Southeast). These quality differences likely reflect spending differences; the Southeast spends five times as much per ECE student as does the North, and more than six times as much as the Northeast.

Municipalities with higher income and more income inequality are less likely to expand investment in early child education. A study of Brazil's over 5,000 municipalities during 1995–2008 demonstrates two key points about municipal characteristics and ECE investment. First, public creches and pre-schools do not benefit all citizens equally. They disproportionately benefit poorer citizens, since the poor are most likely to use these public services. Rich families tend to enroll their children in private ECE, and therefore are less invested in the public education system. Second, the distribution of income in a municipality hugely affects public ECE investment. Given extra revenue, poor and equal municipalities are more likely to expand public ECE than are richer and more unequal municipalities. For example, if the municipality with median inequality is given enough new revenue to expand ECE and enroll 100 new children, more unequal municipalities given the same amount of money will enroll fewer than 100 children, and more equal municipalities will enroll more than 100 children, as illustrated in figure 4. Likewise, if the municipality with median income is given enough new revenue to expand ECE and enroll 100 new children, richer municipalities given the same amount of money will enroll fewer than 100 children, and poorer municipalities will enroll more than 100 children.

This is an important finding given the many efforts over the last two decades to transfer money between municipalities in order to partially equalize access to education resources. FUNDEB has explicitly aimed to equalize funding for ECE by guaranteeing all municipalities a minimum amount per child enrolled. Policy makers can better design future education finance reforms by taking into account that not all municipalities have the same incentives to invest additional revenue in ECE. Targeting funds at poor and equal municipalities means the funds are more likely to end up in ECE rather than in higher levels of education or in goods other than education, like public infrastructure. These findings imply that FUNDEB would create better incentives for investment in ECE if it were a national rather than a within-state redistribution.

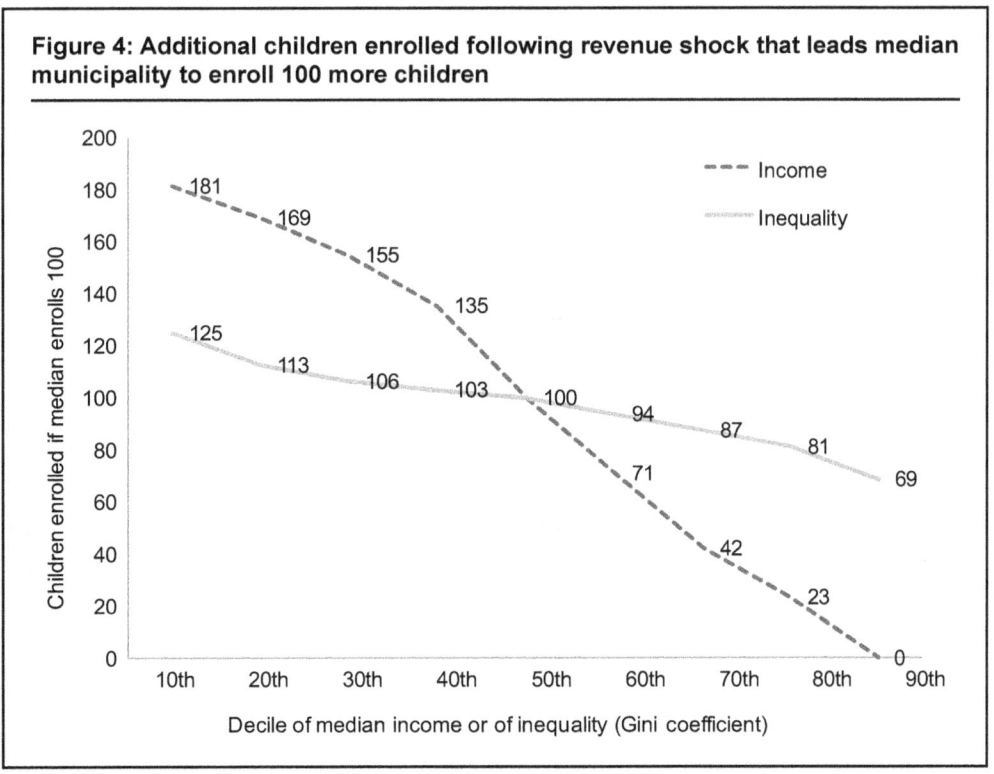

Figure 4: Additional children enrolled following revenue shock that leads median municipality to enroll 100 more children

Source: Kosec (2011), using data from Censo Escolar (1995–2008), Tesouro Nacional (1995–2008), and IBGE Censo (2000).

Much innovation in ECE in Brazil is taking place at the municipal level, providing models within the country to improve both access to and quality of ECE services. Many municipalities are investing in their ECE programs by developing specialized curricula, monitoring systems, improved training for caregivers, and more. With over 5,000 municipalities across Brazil, there is great opportunity for these municipalities to learn from each other to enhance quality and efficiency. Some public programs target specific areas of interest; their curricula may be of interest to other municipalities. For example, the Municipality of Santarém (State of Pará) has developed the program Eco-Schools, which provides lessons about the environment beginning in ECE. Likewise, the Municipality of Rio de Janeiro has developed a curriculum to provide training to parents of creche children that spans education, health, and social assistance. The curriculum includes DVDs, workbooks, and discussion guides. The State of Acre's program of home-based education visits includes workbooks and educational agent guides which demonstrate—both to the agents and then to the parents—how to use common objects available near the home as tools of cognitive stimulation. Clearly, these programs and others like them represent a potent educational resource for other municipalities.

The Policy Implications

Brazil will need to be strategic in where it invests in ECE and use creative models to reach more children. A 2009 constitutional amendment lowered the mandatory school starting age to four years old, and the nation has a stated goal of achieving universal coverage by 2016. Given the 1.6 million pre-school aged children not in pre-school, roll-out must be strategic to reach that goal. In areas of lower population density, ECE centers may need to be constructed on a smaller-than-typical scale, or home visits and other delivery modalities may need to be used in order to cost-effectively satisfy needs for ECE. In some rural areas, it is hard to justify center-based education since sparse population densities would mean that very young children would have to travel very far to fill a creche or pre-school. For example, in the municipality of São Paulo, 0.4 square kilometers of territory would be sufficient to fill an average-sized São Paulo pre-school with 4–5 year olds. However, in more rural Barra do Turvo municipality, also in São Paulo state, over 320 square kilometers would be required to fill an average-sized São Paulo pre-school. Programs such as the State of Acre's Asas de Florestanhia Infantil (for pre-school aged children) or Rio Grande do Sul's Primeira Infância Melhor (for younger children) serve as models for potential alternative outreach. In addition to providing stimulation for children, they provide training to parents to reinforce the benefits from external attention.

Municipalities should better target new centers and spaces at the poorest children (whose parents are not able to self-finance ECE) and open new centers in areas that will achieve this purpose. Among children from the richest fifth of families in Brazil who attend creches, almost 20 percent use publicly-provided creches (figures 5 and 6). If those spaces were instead allocated to the poorest fifth, then their overall enrollment rate in creche would increase by 50 percent. This inefficient targeting of scarce spaces has not improved over time; reliance on public creches by the richest has hovered around 20 percent in the decade since 2002. Furthermore, evidence presented earlier demonstrates that the returns to ECE are particularly high for the poorest and most vulnerable households. These households have the fewest resources to fund alternatives to public creche care.

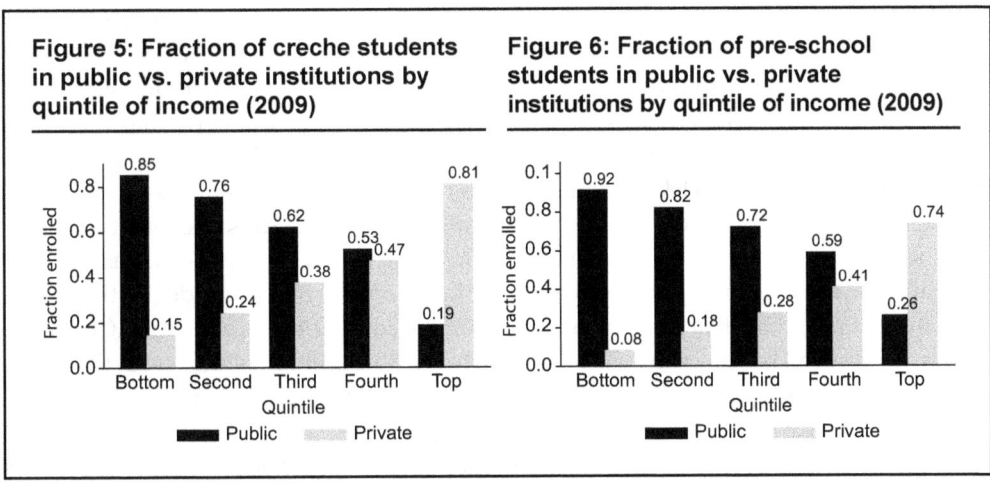

Source: Pesquisa Nacional por Amostra de Domicilios (PNAD), 2009.

By taking advantage of existing Brazilian data (the IBGE's PNAD household survey and demographic census), municipalities can determine which areas have the highest concentrations of low-income households and the least coverage of ECE services. Another solution is allocating existing creche spaces by progressive methods that target vulnerable children in the face of excess demand.

Municipalities should consider the fairest, most transparent methods of allocating public ECE spaces, including a centralized, means-based selection process or a lottery, rather than leaving the decision to individual creche directors. Most municipalities currently allocate spaces via a completely decentralized process in which each creche director is responsible for assigning spaces—usually with official guidelines to prioritize vulnerable children. The disadvantage of this system is that directors may fail to be objective, or they may even be biased against children with special needs or other difficulties, whose care may be more difficult or expensive. A second method, less used in Brazil but more efficient from a resource allocation standpoint, is to have a centralized, means-tested selection process at the municipal level. Using eligibility for a cash-transfer program such as *Bolsa Família* or data from the social protection register *(Cadastro Único)* can facilitate placement of children with the greatest need for public assistance. A third method, which the Municipality of Rio de Janeiro adopted for cohorts entering creches from 2008 through 2010, is to use a lottery to assign scarce spaces among equally eligible families. An advantage of the lottery is that it provides every interested child with the possibility of a space. Because no testing of children's socioeconomic status is perfect, this means that even children who are judged to be less vulnerable by standard indicators but who perhaps have some particular, less visible needs have the possibility of gaining a place. This also leads to more diversity in socioeconomic background across creche children. Either a means-tested or a lottery system leads to greater transparency and fairness than allocation based on director discretion. Both methods require the development of reliable information systems to track children from their first entry into the education system.

Teachers need specific guidance on the best stimulation activities to use in the classroom, to complement existing ECE curricular guidelines. Teachers at Brazilian ECE centers rate relatively high on interactions, suggesting that these teachers are motivated to engage with children. But Brazilian ECE centers rate very poorly on effective activities for stimulating children's cognitive and social development. Teachers lack strong guidance on effective activities. A valuable next step will be to build on the Ministry of Education's 1988 three-volume curricular guide for ECE and the curricular directives laid out by the National Education Council in 2009. Specifically, providing practical workbooks or guides with lesson plans containing defined activities in pre-reading, pre-mathematics, and other areas will help educators not only understand what activities are effective, but also how to implement them. Some municipalities—such as the Municipality of Rio de Janeiro—are developing their own curricular guides with specific guidance on program structure and activities. These could serve as a model. ECE educators will also need hands-on training (i.e., not merely a seminar held far from their own classroom on how to teach more effectively) and careful supervision by experienced, effective ECE educators.

The federal government should encourage strong municipal monitoring systems that hold ECE institutions accountable for their results, introduce a standard observational tool, and provide licensing guidelines for minimum quality standards that municipalities can adapt. The Ministry of Education has set minimum standards of infrastructure quality for creches and pre-schools. The next step will be to establish additional licensing guidelines regarding child-caregiver ratios and caregiver qualifications. Municipalities can greatly improve quality by introducing standardized observational tools, such as the ITERS-R and ECERS-R instruments, to allow for regular, systematic monitoring of activity quality and program structure. In some international systems, ECE observational results are published so that parents can use quality data to choose the best centers for their children and policy makers can use the same data to target lower-quality centers for improvement interventions. The Municipality of Rio de Janeiro recently introduced testing of child cognitive development in all creches. Results (concealing individual child profiles) have been used to identify the creches most successful in stimulating development, to promote cross-creche learning.

Brazil should facilitate knowledge sharing across ECE providers, so that they can learn from one another's success stories. Given the great array of experimentation and innovation at the municipal level, the Ministry of Education can encourage knowledge sharing on a number of levels. Several networks for early child development (ECD) exist: the National Network for Early Childhood focuses principally on improving national policy; the National Union of Municipal Education Leaders (UNDIME) likewise disseminates some documents on national early education policy. Recently, two initiatives for more direct sharing of information have been launched. One is the Network for Cooperation and Peace for Children, which is a social networking site (a là Facebook) where policy makers, nonprofit workers, educators, and other interested citizens actively share information. A second initiative launched by the National Forum for Early Child Development and the World Bank, called the Network for Cooperation in Early Child Development, seeks to provide a map of ECD services across Brazil. It has also developed a social networking site focused on sharing exactly the kinds of materials described above: information on innovative programs, experiences, and best practices. An initiative that the federal government formerly sponsored is an annual Prize for Quality in Early Child Education, which ran from 2000 through 2005 and highlighted innovative projects implemented by individual municipalities or ECE centers. These kinds of programs can help municipalities learn from one another.

Integrating health services into creches and pre-schools can provide opportunities to improve child welfare in cost-effective ways, and would be facilitated by establishing a cross-sectoral coordinating agency. Multisectoral programs help parents learn about and access in one place all of the services they need to help their children flourish, rather than having to separately seek out services about which they may be unaware. The most established example of cross-sectoral collaboration in ECD in Brazil is the Rio Grande do Sul program, Primeira Infância Melhor. Although the program is housed in the State Health Secretariat, it is managed by the State Technical Group, which includes technical staff from the Secretariats of Health, Education, Culture, Justice, and Social Development, regional coordinators from health and education from across the state, and others. The education secretariats in the State of Acre, the Municipality of Rio de Janeiro, and elsewhere in Brazil are working to establish partnerships with health secretariats to offer these comprehensive services in a single locale. Brazil has made progress in this regard through the development of the National Plan for Early Childhood, prepared collaboratively by the National Network for Early Childhood. But if the Government of Brazil is serious about cross-sectoral collaboration on ECD, it will need to establish a coordinating agency to oversee its implementation.

Partnerships outside the public sector can provide significant resources to expand ECD services, improve their quality, and innovate in reaching the most vulnerable populations. Data from 2009 show that the private sector provides more than one third of creche spaces: 29 percent are fully private and 14 percent are *conveniado* (or government contracted). Likewise, a quarter of provision at the pre-school level is through the private sector: 19 percent fully private and 5 percent *conveniado*. The number of *conveniado* centers is growing rapidly, with hundreds of early child institutions contracted each year. This expansion signals significant capacity in the private sector to supplement the efforts of the public sector in providing early child services. Furthermore, the data on quality suggest that contracted institutions have better infrastructure on average than public institutions and are not distinguishably different in other observable measures from either fully private or fully public ECE centers. Expansion of contractual relationships with careful, ongoing monitoring of quality might help the government satisfy immediate demands for ECE. Although FUNDEB reimbursements are equal for public and *conveniado* spaces, municipalities have the liberty to compensate *conveniado* spaces at higher or lower levels, providing the freedom to create incentives for private provision for difficult-to-reach populations, as has taken place in Chile. In addition to subsidized provision through the private sector, Brazil may also benefit from expanding its use of public-private partnerships to offset some of the budget impacts of coverage expansion and quality improvements. Many corporations have a philanthropic arm which can contribute to ECD, and a number of corporations across Brazil are already doing this. In many countries, these partnerships are mobilized to provide matching funds to provide and improve ECD services.

Using participatory budgeting (PB) to distribute educational resources has the potential to lead to more equitable outcomes and to target resources at the poorest children. Participatory budgeting began in Porto Alegre, Brazil, and has since spread to many municipalities across the country. It allows citizens to vote on how to use a share of municipal revenue designated for their neighborhood, and to elect neighborhood representatives to make municipality-wide spending decisions. Additionally, policy makers must publicize budgets and expenditures to promote transparency. PB increases political participation of marginalized groups and can lead to more pro-poor expenditures, including public investment in ECE. It does so by ensuring that the poor—who have the highest demand for public ECE—are more directly and fully involved in decision-making. Resulting policies are more likely to reflect the will of the people rather than the preferences of the most politically-powerful citizens. The federal government may wish to encourage and create incentives for PB as a part of a broader early child education policy. The government could even create incentives for more limited forms of PB that specifically apply only to education spending.

CHAPTER 1

Early Child Education—A Top Priority for the Coming Years

The year 2011 marked the beginning of a new administration in Brazil. The Ministry of Education clearly identified early child education (ECE) as one of the top priorities of the new administration, along with secondary school and improving the reputation of the teaching profession (Weber 2011).[1] Within early child education, the Ministry of Education identified two key priorities: expanding access to creches (centers for children ages 0–3) and pre-schools (ages 4–5), and improving their quality. Brazil has made great advances on both fronts in the past two decades, but the quality of service delivery must improve, and major gaps remain in reaching the poor.

Fifteen years ago, less than half of Brazil's children aged four to six were enrolled in pre-school, and fewer than one in twelve attended creche. A scant one in five pre-school teachers had training beyond secondary school. Now, the number of children in pre-school has increased by more than fifty percent, to 75 percent of 4–5 year-olds and 81 percent of 4–6 year-olds; moreover, 18 percent of 0–3 year-olds attend creche, and half of pre-school teachers have post-secondary training.[2] School infrastructure has also improved steadily, and class sizes have declined.

At the same time, these numbers indicate that many children still do not attend pre-school—compulsory since 2009—and most do not attend creche.[3] The poorest children stand to benefit the most from both early education opportunities and the income gains of having an additional working parent, but only one in nine of these children attend a creche. This exacerbates existing income gaps. Recent in-depth studies of creches and pre-schools across Brazil also reveal that their quality lags far behind that found in higher-income countries.

Early child development interventions are essential to both increasing the productivity of Brazil as a whole and to providing equitable opportunities for the disadvantaged. These programs benefit the poor more than other populations, and the poor are most in need of these benefits. Education interventions are crucial. Creches and pre-schools provide opportunities for stimulation and development that can wire children for future success. For these centers to be effective, however, they must satisfy certain quality standards, and expose children to the right types of activities and experiences.

Why Are Early Child Development and Early Child Education So Important?

The first few years of a child's life hold massive sway over long-term outcomes. From birth to age five, children develop "foundational capabilities" on which the rest of their development builds. Just as positive environments and opportunities can wire children for success, failure to provide those opportunities can significantly reduce future opportunities (Shonkoff and Phillips 2000). Children's health, wealth, and home environment have a major impact on many long-term outcomes, putting poor children at high risk for slower development. For example, researchers examined vocabulary test scores for Ecuadorian children between three and six years old (Paxson and Schady 2007). They found that while rich and poor children had very similar vocabulary test scores at three years of age, those scores had diverged dramatically by age six, when the poorest 25 percent had only two-thirds the vocabulary of the richest 25 percent (figure 1.1).

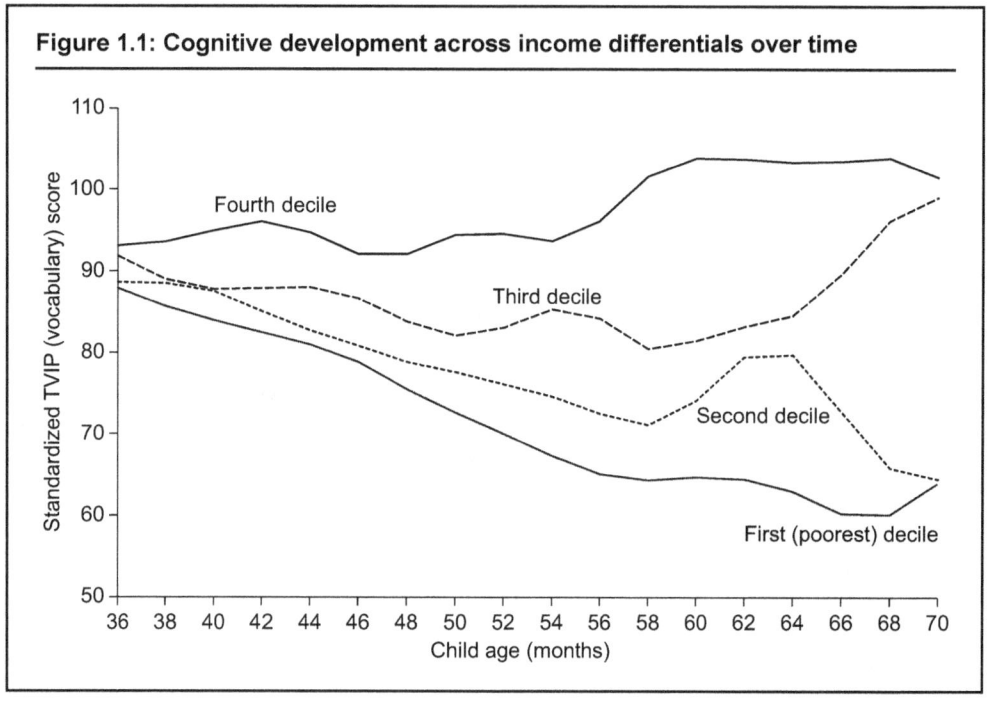

Source: Paxson and Schady (2007).

While this evidence demonstrates that children from different backgrounds are on different trajectories, the encouraging news is that public interventions have been shown to mitigate the effects of unfavorable circumstances. Conditional cash transfer programs such as Bolsa Familia have improved children's schooling and health. Certain home visiting programs and parent training programs have led to not only improved health, but also a reduction in crime and other adverse behaviors when children reach adolescence. Several child care and pre-school programs have had long-term impacts on health, education, employment, income, and other indicators of well-being (Almond and Currie 2011). Likewise, much of the evidence on early child development demonstrates that impacts are particularly effective for poor children, leading Economics Nobel laureate James Heckman to argue that "investing in disadvantaged young children is a rare public policy with no equity-efficiency tradeoff" (Heckman and Masterov 2007).

The importance of early child education

No single area of investment—be it education, health, home environment, or child protection—is sufficient to ensure the success of Brazil's children. Children need a range of investments in different areas. But education and cognitive stimulation interventions—

whether through center-based care or through parent training and home-based stimulation—have enormous potential to make a difference for children. Reviews of early child development programs show that interventions targeting one area have large spillover effects in other areas. Nutrition programs have been shown to affect cognitive development, conditional cash transfer programs have improved health, and education and child care interventions affect health and behavior (Almond and Currie 2011). However, in a review of thirty early child development interventions around the world, researchers found that those interventions which provided education services or a combination of education and nutrition services tended to have better impacts on children's cognitive development than those that provided nutritional or financial transfers alone (Nores and Barnett 2010). For example, a program in Jamaica combined cognitive stimulation with nutritional supplementation and found that—sixteen years later—the cognitive stimulation cut high school dropout rates in half, whereas the supplementation had no impact (Walker et al. 2005). Likewise, an integrated program coordinating home-based and center-based cognitive stimulation and nutritional supplements in the Philippines had major impacts on cognitive outcomes and on some health outcomes (Armecin et al. 2006). In both cases, early child education was critical.

Center-based pre-schools and creches have relatively high start-up costs, but provide clear opportunities to add other child care programs (such as nutrition monitoring and supplementation or parental education) at low additional cost. That is, formal early child education can create opportunities for a multitude of successful interventions. The constantly expanding array of evidence points to enduring impacts of early child care and education programs around the world, although with two important qualifications. First and most importantly, having a program is no guarantee of success: quality is essential, and low quality programs can be worse than no program at all. Second, the strongest evidence comes from programs targeting the most vulnerable. The evidence for this impact comes from around the globe: the United States, Europe, Asia, Latin America, and—increasingly—Brazil itself.

Significant and lasting positive impacts from around the world

Rigorous evaluations of high-quality early child education programs have demonstrated long-term impacts on educational attainment, poverty, and participation in crime, as demonstrated in figure 1.2. The strongest evidence comes from the United States, where evaluations of early child education programs such as the High/Scope Perry Pre-school program, the Abecedarian program, and the Chicago Parent Child program have demonstrated long-term impacts on a wide range of outcomes. The Perry Pre-school program has an estimated social return of 7–10 percent, which is significantly higher than average investments (Heckman et al. 2010). These were relatively small programs: the Perry Pre-school program had 123 original participants, and the Abecedarian program had 56 (Masse and Barnett 2002). However, evidence on Head Start, the largest pre-school program for vulnerable children in the United States (currently serving about 800,000 children each year), suggests positive impacts on cognitive development, grade progression, and college participation, and reductions in crime, depression, other behavioral problems, and even mortality (Almond and Currie 2011). Likewise, large-scale pre-school programs in the United States, Chile, and Argentina have demonstrated positive impacts on children's cognitive development and—sometimes—positive behavioral impacts (figure 1.3).

Figure 1.2: Impact of high-quality, highly targeted early child education programs

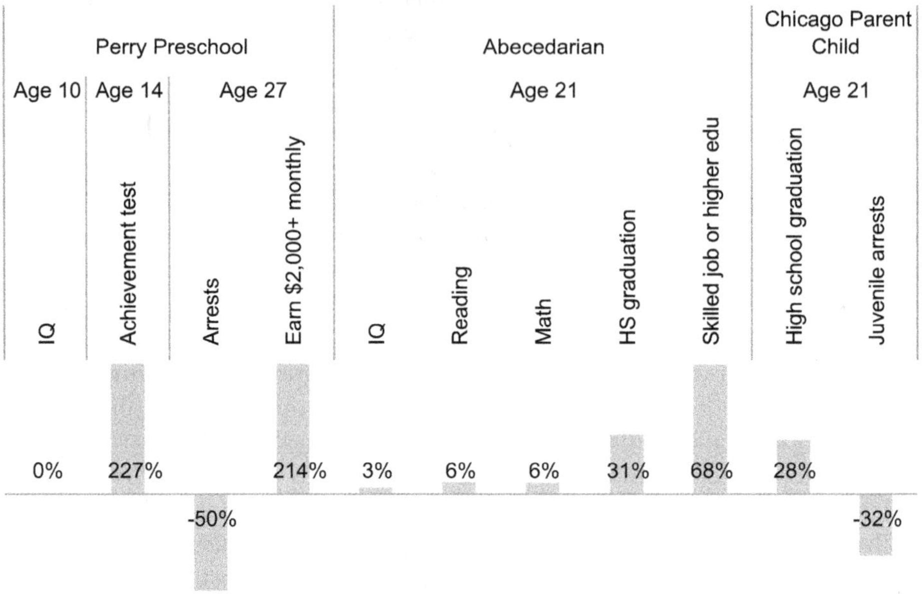

	Perry Preschool			Abecedarian					Chicago Parent Child	
Age 10	Age 14		Age 27	Age 21					Age 21	
IQ	Achievement test	Arrests	Earn $2,000+ monthly	IQ	Reading	Math	HS graduation	Skilled job or higher edu	High school graduation	Juvenile arrests
0%	227%	−50%	214%	3%	6%	6%	31%	68%	28%	−32%

Source: Barnett (2004).

Studies from Brazil—both those using national data and those examining specific municipalities—also demonstrate gains from early child education on short-run cognitive development, medium-run academic performance, and long-run educational attainment and earnings, as demonstrated in table 1.1. (A more complete review of evidence from Brazil is summarized in Appendix B.) However, most studies of the effectiveness of ECD in Brazil have relied on assumptions that children with similar observable income and family background characteristics would experience similar outcomes in the absence of pre-school. This may not be the case; families that look similar may have different

Table 1.1: Sample of Brazilian evidence on impacts of early child education

Sample	Results
Southeast & Northeast	Almost half an additional year of schooling by adulthood Two to six percent increase in future earnings for men (more for those coming from illiterate households)
Campo Grande, Florianópolis, Teresina	Positive significant impact on *Provinha Brasil* (second grade literacy) results, particularly for children who attended high-quality pre-schools
Sertãozinho	*Provinha Brasil* results 6% higher for children who attended ECE
Rio de Janeiro	Positive impacts of high-quality creche participation on mental and social development while still in creche
Nationally representative	Positive impact of creche participation on fourth-grade math scores

Sources: The Southeast & Northeast study comes from Young (2001). The Campo Grande, Florianópolis, and Teresina study comes from Fundação Carlos Chagas (2010). The Sertãozinho evidence comes from Felício, Menezes, and Zoghbi (2010). The national study is Rodrigues, Pinto, and Santos (2010).

unmeasured qualities, such as their commitment to education, which contribute to child outcomes independently of pre-school. Still, the Brazil data generally points to positive returns to participation in early child education, from the time of the intervention (in a Rio de Janeiro study), to primary school outcomes (in several studies), to outcomes in adulthood (in a study in the Northeast and Southeast). The most credible evidence from the United States, in contrast, comes from studies which use randomized provision of ECE and rigorous evaluation methods.

Quality of early child education matters

Providing a child with a place in a center or program is insufficient to confer the promised returns of early child education. Recent studies show that the set of cognitive and non-cognitive skills children acquire at school is much more relevant to longer-term life outcomes than is schooling attainment (Hanushek and Woessman 2008). In Brazil and elsewhere, higher quality ECE centers lead to better cognitive development.

A variety of studies have used observational instruments to rate the quality of creches (for children 0–3 years old) and pre-schools (for children 4–5 years old) according to infrastructure, activities, interactions between staff and children, and so on. For example, a recent study examined pre-schools in three municipalities (Campo Grande, Florianópolis, and Teresina) across 43 measures of quality and then linked the findings to students' second-grade reading scores. A high-quality pre-school would have—for example—a well-lit main space, good supervision of child safety, books, puzzles, and small blocks for fine motor skill development, affectionate and respectful caregivers, a daily routine that includes both individual time and small-group activities, and regular information provision to parents. A lower quality pre-school would lack most of these characteristics. After controlling for some observable differences between students, the study showed that children who attended higher quality pre-schools did much better on their second grade reading exam. In fact, the difference in reading scores between children attending a higher quality pre-school and those attending a lower quality pre-school was even larger than the difference between children with a mother who had finished secondary school and those without. The test scores of children who attended a low-quality pre-school were not significantly better than those of children who did not attend pre-school at all (Fundação Carlos Chagas 2010). Of course, there may be other, unobservable student and family characteristics that explain both the selection of a high-quality pre-school and student performance. However, these results are strongly suggestive that the quality of a pre-school (and not merely attendance) determines student outcomes.

Evidence at the creche level reveals analogous results. In 2001, researchers used similar observational instruments in 100 creches around Rio de Janeiro, and looked at the association between creche quality and children's cognitive, social, and physical development. Overall development of children in the highest quality creches was significantly higher than in the worst creches, particularly in terms of social and cognitive development. Importantly, the authors also note that improvements in the quality of activities and in program structure are relatively inexpensive ways to enhance the quality of early child education (Barros et al. 2011a). In contrast, other kinds of investments such as infrastructure improvements had no impact on child development for the same group of creches. Thus, investing in quality—and identifying the most needed elements of quality—has large payoffs. In Chapter Three, we use this quality analysis to inform the quantity-quality trade-offs municipal governments must make.

The results of these Brazilian studies complement international studies from the United States, Canada, and elsewhere, demonstrating that high-quality center-based care makes a huge difference, and showing that low-quality center-based care can be worse for development than home care.[4] In one study from the United States, children in low-quality programs performed worse on post-tests than on pre-tests of social and behavioral skills, motivation, and self control after one school year, while children in medium- and high-quality programs improved (Thornburg et al. 2009).[5] Brazil cannot afford to merely provide spaces in child care centers. It must provide quality.

Impacts for vulnerable children

While there is evidence for the importance of center-based early child stimulation and education for all children, the impacts seem to be greatest for vulnerable children. Vulnerable children come from poor families with relatively low levels of parental education, and receive relatively less cognitive stimulation and exposure to vocabulary at home. In the absence of interventions, these children are at a great disadvantage, and that disadvantage expands over time. As in Ecuador (figure 1.1), evidence from the United States shows that the gap between the highest and the lowest income quintiles in terms of both social skills and school preparation (reading and math) is significant upon school entry: children in the lowest income quintile have math scores 20 percent lower than children in the highest income quintile (Barnett, Brown and Shore 2004). The vulnerable children are just beginning their school career, and they are already far behind more privileged children.

Therefore, early child education can particularly benefit the poor, helping to close the gap in cognitive development across income groups. A World Bank study compares adults from two regions of Brazil (the Northeast and the Southeast) who attended pre-school to those who did not and found that pre-school attendance is associated with additional total years of education. However, individuals benefitted more from pre-school if their parents were illiterate than if their parents had four years of schooling. Pre-school was associated with 0.4 additional years of lifetime educational attainment for those whose parents had four years of schooling, and with 0.6 additional years for those whose parents were illiterate (Young 2001). Other evidence from programs in the United States, the United Kingdom, Nepal, Vietnam, Guatemala, and elsewhere confirms that many early child development programs have particularly high impacts for the most vulnerable (Engle et al. 2007).

On the other hand, the more ambiguous evidence on early child education programs comes from universal programs, where vulnerable children are not targeted. A large-scale pre-school program in Canada (Quebec) showed small but negative impacts on children's health and behavioral development when the program was expanded to middle-class children who would otherwise have been at home with a parent (Baker, Gruber and Milligan 2008; Almond and Currie 2011). Likewise, a universally-available pre-school program in Denmark showed no impacts (Gupta and Simonsen 2010). To be sure, some universal programs have shown positive effects on average (figure 1.3), but these findings are less consistent than are those for the most vulnerable children.

These findings highlight two key reasons to target the poorest, most vulnerable children in providing early child education. First, early child education programs show the most consistent returns for vulnerable children. These children are least likely to receive adequate cognitive and non-cognitive development at home, and least likely to be enrolled in private early child education. Second, these vulnerable children are most likely

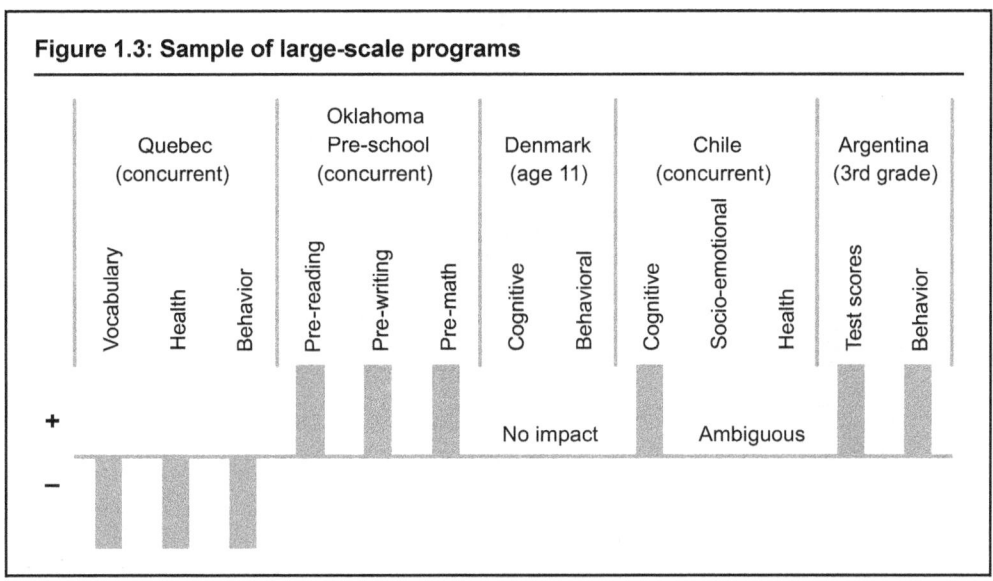

Sources: The Quebec findings come from Baker, Gruber, and Milligan (2008). The Oklahoma findings are from Gormley and Gayer (2006). The Denmark findings are from Gupta and Simonsen (2010). The Chile findings are from Urzúa and Veramendi (2011). The Argentina findings are from Berlinski, Galiani, and Gertler (2009).

to enter school with a significant deficit, so there are equity reasons to target them and allow them to catch up. Brazil's policy for pre-school is that it be universal and compulsory, but it will take several years to achieve this (80 percent were enrolled in 2009), and municipalities will have until 2016 to come into compliance. Creche access will not be universal for the foreseeable future (18 percent were enrolled in 2009). Policies that target the most vulnerable are the most likely to raise enrollment and to cost-effectively improve child outcomes.

How Has Brazil Advanced in Early Child Development and Early Child Education in Recent Years?

The situation of young children in Brazil has improved significantly in recent decades, in terms of government policy, government programs, and—most importantly—child outcomes. These gains can be observed across sectors, since child policy spans education, health, legal protections, water, sanitation, and other areas.

Government policy advances

Brazil's government policy over the last 20 years can broadly be characterized as pro-child.[6] The Federal Constitution of 1988 declared children to be citizens and identified the Ministry of Education as responsible for the education of children ages 0–6. The 1990 Statute for Children and Youth clarified children's rights to education, to a family or guardianship, and to protection from labor and from full penalties for crimes. Other laws in more specific areas have improved life for children. The Law for Free Civil Registry (1997) eliminated any fee associated with birth registration, which is essential for helping children take advantage of social programs.[7] In health, the National Pact to Reduce Maternal and Neonatal Mortality[8] (2004) and the National Policy on Food and Nutrition[9] (1999) have also advanced the state of children.

Table 1.2: Policy changes in early child education in Brazil

Year	Law	Policy change
1975	Pre-school Education Coordinating Body (Coordenação de Educação Pré-Escolar)	Education of 4–6 year olds put under responsibility of MEC
1988	Federal Constitution (Art 208.IV)	Defined ECE (age 0–6) as government responsibility
1996	Law of Directives and Bases of National Education	Placed responsibility for ECE in municipalities Defined ECE (age 0–6) as part of Basic Education Set starting age for obligatory education at 7
1998	Fundamental Education Fund (FUNDEF)	Increased education revenue to municipalities
2005	Law 11.114	Lowered obligatory starting age to 6
2006	National Policy for Early Child Education	Defined strategies and goals for ECE at each level of government
2007	Basic Education Fund (FUNDEB)	Provided municipalities with capitation grants for ECE starting from birth
2009	Constitutional Amendment 59	Lowered obligatory starting age to 4

Source: Compiled by authors.

Over the last 30 years, Brazil has made policy advances in early child education (table 1.2), and these advances are clearly linked to expansions in programs to benefit children. The precursor to these was the 1975 establishment of the Pre-School Education Coordinating Body, which put the education of 4–6 year olds under the responsibility of the Ministry of Education, or MEC (Ministério de Educação 2006). Next came the Federal Constitution of 1988, which squarely identified early child education as a responsibility of the government—specifically, the Ministry of Education. Then, the Law of Directives and Bases of National Education (LDB) of 1996 gave municipal governments the responsibility for ECE and made age seven the starting age for compulsory education. LDB also defined ECE as part of basic education, continuing a transition of creches (0–3) from the Ministry of Social Development to the Ministry of Education that stemmed from the 1988 constitution but had not been completed in practice. A 2005 amendment to the LDB reduced the compulsory education starting age to six, and a 2009 constitutional amendment reduced it to four, making Brazil's starting age among the youngest in the world (table 1.3).

The transition of creches to the purview of the Ministry of Education is essential in viewing them not as a holding place while mothers work, but rather as a place of education. The transition has been a slow one, signaled by the fact that an inter-ministry commission was established as late as 2005 to propose the transition of creches and preschools still supported through the Ministry of Social Development to the Ministry of

Table 1.3: Starting age for compulsory education in Europe, North America, and selected other countries

Age	Countries
3	Mexico
4	Brazil, Northern Ireland
5	Argentina, Greece, Hungary, Latvia, Malta, the Netherlands, England (UK), Scotland (UK)
6	Austria, Belgium, Canada, Chile, Cuba, Denmark, France, Germany, Hong Kong SAR, China; Iceland, Ireland, Italy, Norway, Poland, Republic of Korea, Romania, Singapore, Slovak Republic, Slovenia, Spain, Turkey, United States*
7	Bulgaria, Estonia, Finland, Lithuania, Sweden

Source: Eurydice (n.d.) and UNESCO Institute for Statistics. Mexico: Yoshikawa et al. (2007).
Note: *True in two thirds of states in the United States.

Education. This was also one of the priorities highlighted in January of 2011 by Minister of Education Fernando Haddad (Paraguassu 2011).

A major legislative effort to ensure sufficient municipal investments in basic education (primary and lower-secondary school) was the Fund for the Development of Elementary Education and Teacher Development (FUNDEF), implemented in 1998. The law did not target early child education, but it made additional education revenue available to many municipalities, potentially freeing funds for early child education. The law mandated that all municipal and state governments contribute 15 percent of their revenue from four existing intergovernmental transfers to a state-level fund.[10] This resulted in 27 education funds: one for each state and one for the Federal District. The money in each fund was redistributed to contributors according to their share of the state's enrolled public primary and lower-secondary school students. All receipts from the fund had to be spent on education, and 60 percent had to be spent on teacher compensation. Each municipality established a council to oversee expenditures. If fund receipts alone did not reach a federal minimum per enrolled student, the federal government would top-off the fund, bringing it up to the required level.[11]

FUNDEF laid the groundwork for further education finance reforms that had much more direct impacts on early child education. In June 2005, Congress voted on a bill proposing the Fund for the Maintenance and Development of Basic Education (FUNDEB). This reform proposal extended the provisions of FUNDEF to also cover pre-school students, thus ensuring municipal governments a minimum amount of funding per enrolled pre-school child. Initially, the FUNDEB proposal excluded children enrolled in creche. The Brazilian Congress' Select Committee charged with reviewing FUNDEB then decided to additionally include children enrolled in creche, and a vote on the floor of Congress eventually confirmed their inclusion (Campos, Fullgraf and Wiggers 2006). The FUNDEB law was implemented in 2007.[12] In its final form, FUNDEB modified FUNDEF's redistribution algorithm to take into account total creche, pre-school, primary, and secondary school students (MEC 2008). It also gradually increased the fraction of revenue paid into the state-level funds.[13] This created clear, new incentives for municipalities to invest in early child education.

Improvements in government programs

Public investment in programs for children and adolescents in Brazil doubled between 2006 and 2009 (figure 1.4). Some of the most far-reaching and high-profile interventions are the social assistance programs that also benefit education and health, Bolsa Escola and Bolsa Alimentação, which combined to become Bolsa Familia in 2003. Coverage of children ages 0 to 7 by Bolsa Familia rose from 3.7 million to 6.2 million children between 2005 and 2010 (Ministério da Saúde do Brasil n.d.).

Child outcome improvements

These policies and programs have truly borne fruit. In the last decade, unregistered births in Brazil dropped by 60 percent, from 30 percent in 1995 to about 10 percent in 2007 (Muzzi 2010). In health, the proportion of stunted children under age five (i.e., extremely low height-for-age) has fallen from 14 percent in 1996 to just 7 percent in 2007.[14] Likewise, child mortality among under-five children and infant mortality (under age one) have both dropped by almost two-thirds over a decade. While cognitive development of young children is not measured on a wide scale, participation in ECE programs has in-

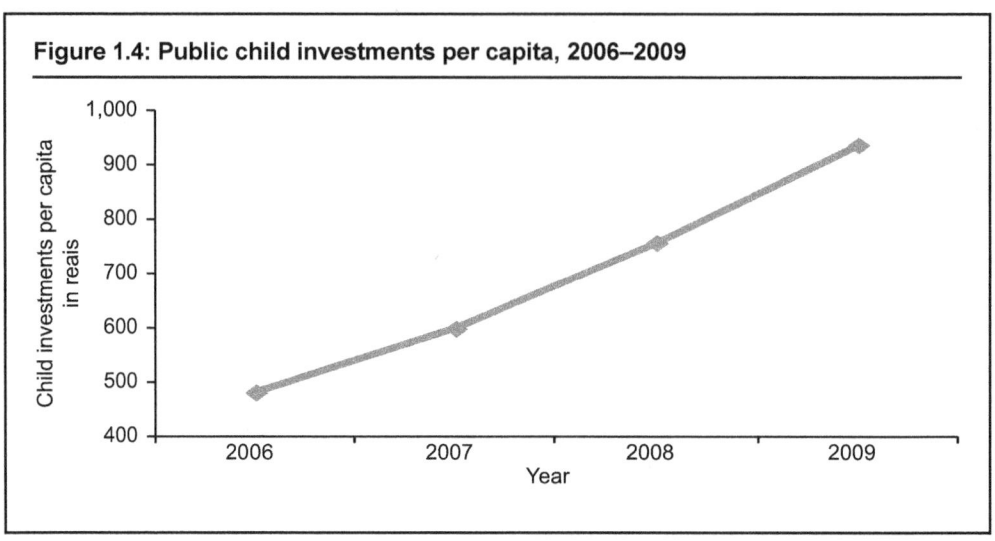

Figure 1.4: Public child investments per capita, 2006–2009

Source: UNICEF (n.d.).

creased dramatically, reaching 18 percent of children ages 0–3 and 80 percent of children ages 4–6 in 2009.

While Brazil has made a great deal of progress on early child development policy in recent years, in some ways it still lags in early child outcomes. Child health is a major concern, with high mortality and medium stunting rates. Brazil has an under-five mortality rate that is in the middle of the range for Latin American countries, but the highest for middle income Latin American countries. In 2007, Argentina, Chile, Colombia, Costa Rica, Mexico, Uruguay, and República Bolivariana de Venezuela all had lower under-five mortality rates than did Brazil, while most of the other (poorer) Latin American countries had higher mortality rates (table 1.4). Early child education enrollment in Brazil is high relative to countries in the region, but still not comparable to that found in the richest nations, as will be discussed in detail in Chapter 3.

Table 1.4: Child health outcomes across the world in 2007

Region	Mortality rate per 1,000 population (under 5)	Stunting rate (%) (under 5)	GDP per capita, PPP*
Brazil	23	7%	$9,181
Colombia	20	—	$8,084
Mexico	19	16%†	$13,371
Latin America and Caribbean	25	16%	$9,712
United States	8	4%‡	$43,662
Sweden	3	—	$34,782
OECD	9	—	$30,860

Sources: World Bank World Development Indicators; UNICEF State of the World's Children.
Note: * GDP is purchasing power parity (i.e., adjusted for spending power in different environments), in constant 2005 International dollars.
† 2006 data (2007 data unavailable)
‡ 2004 data (2007 data unavailable)
— Not applicable.

This report, in addition to examining Brazilian data and policy over time, draws on data from a variety of international comparisons. Some of them are comparable to Brazil in income (such as Colombia and Mexico), others in scope of population (such as the United States and Mexico), and some in terms of urbanization and population density (Sweden). All have expanded or improved their early child education systems in recent years and provide insights on which Brazil can draw. The report also highlights innovative practices from elsewhere in the world that are relevant to Brazil's challenges.

Key Issues Facing Brazil in Early Child Education

Despite many improvements in early child education, including strengthening some elements of quality and expansions in access, Brazil has essential issues to resolve if it seeks to close the opportunity gap and make long-term, high-return investments in Brazil's children. This report explores each of these issues in detail.

How to provide world-class early child education, especially in the most difficult locations

Research on early child education centers across Brazil demonstrates both that the quality of the center has a massive impact on child development and that quality is sorely lacking in many creches and pre-schools. While infrastructure quality and teacher qualifications have steadily improved, the quality of activities is still deficient. In addition to the broad curricular guides published by MEC in 1998 and the curricular directives laid out by the National Education Council in 2009, teachers need specific guidance on the most stimulating activities. To close the quality gap in early child education, other levels of government should support municipalities with tools for monitoring the quality of activities, for developing specific programs of intellectual and social stimulation, and for holding centers accountable for the quality of their programs. Fundação Carlos Chagas (in partnership with the Ministry of Education and the Inter-American Development Bank) as well as the Institute for Applied Economic Research (IPEA) have already developed tools for evaluating quality. The federal government can also provide clear guidelines for monitoring and licensing ECE centers, ensuring that minimum standards are available for municipalities. Chapter 2 of this report details the evolution of quality in ECE centers in Brazil and the variety of ways that Brazil can strengthen them.

Reaching the children who need these programs the most

High-quality early child education must be extended to children who, to date, have been marginalized. While access has expanded impressively (figure 1.5 below), more than one million children remain out of pre-school, which is now a constitutionally compulsory level of schooling (albeit compliance will not be mandatory until 2016). The poorest children are most in need of these programs, and targeting them should be the government's first priority. However, enrollment for the poorest children is only 67 percent for pre-school and 12 percent for creches. Currently, 13 percent of public creche spaces—which are entirely free to the child—are taken by children from the richest fifth of families, while only 12 percent of poor children are in any creche at all. Brazil must be strategic in where it rolls out ECE in the short run, and creative in how it does so, to ensure that new spaces reach the underserved.

These income-based disparities in access mirror those between rural and urban areas. In rural areas, alternative delivery mechanisms like home visits—as are done in the state of Acre (through education) and in Rio Grande do Sul (through health)—may be

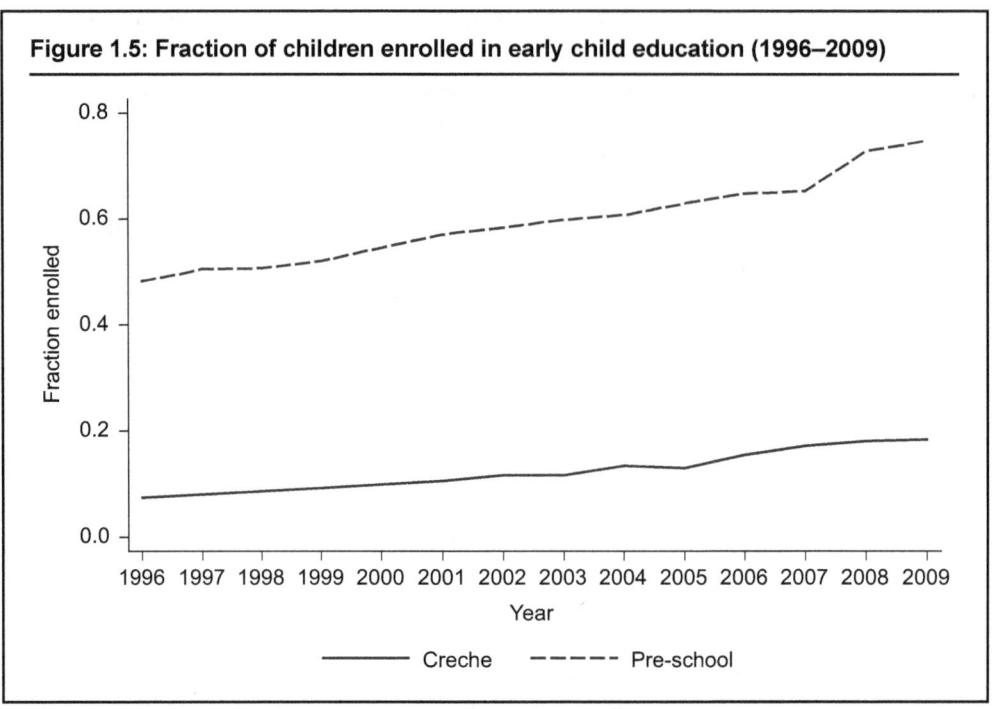

Source: Pesquisa Nacional por Amostra de Domicilios (PNAD), 1996–2009.

the only way to reach the most distant children. Chapter 3 of this report explores ECE coverage in detail and the implications of the coming expansion.

The next steps in ECD for Brazil

While improving quality and expanding coverage are at the top of Brazil's stated agenda for early child development, Chapter Four of this report explores three other areas integral to success in delivering effective ECD services on a large scale.

How to effectively integrate early child development services? Considering areas in ECD, child health is one in which Brazil is weakest relative to comparator countries, whereas coverage in social protection and in education is stronger. The relative strength of education provides an opportunity to bundle services and take advantage of the stronger education infrastructure to provide improved health services for children. Bundling services can improve early child health and cognitive development simultaneously. Evidence shows that combined programs can be highly effective (see, e.g., Nores and Barnett 2010). Examples from Australia, New Zealand, Sweden, and Chile all demonstrate the effectiveness of cross-sectoral child development programs in improving outcomes across sectors. In Brazil, the municipality of Rio de Janeiro, the state of Acre, and the state of Rio Grande do Sul, among others, are experimenting with these kinds of programs.

How to leverage private support? Many other countries have succeeded in incorporating private sector support effectively to provide large-scale ECD services. This can include direct provision, as Brazil does through creches and pre-schools contracted (*conveniado*) by the government. It can also include partnerships to augment public financing—likely essential in the face of Brazil's massive required expansion in coverage.

How to compensate for municipal differences? Although reforms in education spending have created incentives for all municipalities to invest in ECE, poorer children in wealthier and in more unequal municipalities are likely to receive fewer public ECE options because of lesser public commitment to ECE provision. Brazil can take steps, such as encouraging elements of participatory budgeting practices, to protect the poorest children's ECE opportunities everywhere.

Notes

1. In this report, Early Child Development (ECD) refers to all activities intended to promote cognitive, emotional, and behavioral development in children age zero to six. Early Child Education (ECE) refers specifically to those ECD activities under the purview of the Ministry of Education. Thus, creche and pre-school attendance is part of ECE, whereas child nutrition and health care provided at a clinic are part of ECD.
2. These enrollment rates are based on parent reports from the 2009 Pesquisa Nacional por Amostra de Domicilios (PNAD). They are the share of children of the given age range that are enrolled in school—whether in early child education or primary school institutions.
3. While Article 6 of Constitutional Amendment 59/09 made four the compulsory starting age for education, municipalities and states have until 2016 to reach full compliance.
4. The finding of negative outcomes for low-quality center-based care has been among children from higher-income households (see Almond and Currie's discussion of Baker et al. 2008). However, the Brazil findings of no impact of low-quality center-based care applied to a representative sample of pre-school attendees.
5. Another study shows a clear correlation between low quality creches and worse outcomes than no daycare at all (Howes 1990).
6. A more comprehensive summary of these can be found in the National Plan for Early Childhood (Rede Nacional Primeira Infância 2010).
7. Lei da Gratuidade do Registro Civil (No 9.534/1997)
8. Pacto Nacional pela Redução da Mortalidade Materna e Neonatal
9. Política Nacional de Alimentação e Nutrição
10. These four transfers—the state and municipal participation funds (FPE/FPM), the tax on goods and services (ICMS), the export-proportional excise tax (IPIexp), and transfers under the complementary law (LC 87/96)—constituted the majority of revenue for most governments.
11. In 1998, six states received federal top-off: Bahia, Ceará, Maranhão, Pará, Pernambuco, and Piauí. The per-child minimum changed annually. It began to vary with child grade level in 2000 and with school type (rural or urban) in 2005.
12. FUNDEB was created by Constitutional Amendment No. 53/2006 and regulated by Law No. 11.494/2007 and Decree No. 6.253/20071. FUNDEB was established for the period 2007–2020, and effectively replaced FUNDEF.
13. FUNDEB gradually increased state and municipal contributions from their four main transfer revenue sources (FPM/FPE, ICMS, IPIexp, LC 87/96): from 15 percent in 2006 to 16.67 percent in 2007, 18.33 percent in 2008, and 20 percent in 2009 onward. FUNDEB also expanded the list of transfer revenues of which a percentage had to be contributed to the state education fund. These transfer sources included: the tax on inheritance and donations (ITCMD), the motor vehicles tax (IPVA), the 50 percent share of the rural territory tax due to municipalities (ITR), and income tax benefits levied on income paid by the municipalities or the state (IRmuni and IRest). The fraction of these transfers that had to be contributed to the state education fund was 6.67 percent in 2007, 13.33 percent in 2008, and 20 percent in 2009 and onward.
14. Stunting is an indicator of child malnutrition. The population of stunted children under age five is the population of under-five children whose height for age is more than two standard deviations below the median for the international reference population ages 0–59 months. For children up to two years old, height is measured by recumbent (lying down) length. For older children, height is measured while standing. The data are based on the World Health Organization's new child growth standards released in 2006.

CHAPTER 2

Ensuring High Quality Early Child Education for Brazil's Children

As Brazil expands its access to pre-school and creche education, hopefully it will capture the major returns promised to investments in early child development. However, as shown in Chapter One, placing children in early child education establishments of low quality makes no promise of returns. The average quality of early child education in Brazil is low, but some municipalities are delivering quality care. Brazil can improve ECE quality by providing better materials to strengthen activities, encouraging effective monitoring systems which keep ECE institutions accountable for their results, and facilitating knowledge sharing among providers.

Current Quality of Early Child Education in Brazil

Global evidence supports the importance of quality for ECD outcomes, but measuring quality for young children is elusive. Clearly high-quality early child education is the product of many elements: the teacher, the infrastructure, the activities, the hygiene routines, and other factors. At higher levels of education, quality is often measured through value-added indicators of student improvement. However, while there are many tools available for measuring child development at early ages, they are less precise than measures for older children and few systems universally test young children. Also, linking those measures to creche and pre-school incentives can have the perverse effect of leading centers with discretion over enrollment to exclude developmentally-delayed children. As a result, creche and pre-school quality is usually measured with multi-dimensional observational instruments, in which enumerators observe the creche or pre-school in session and characterize its quality across a number of areas.

A 2001 study of 100 creches in Rio de Janeiro demonstrates just how these various elements have an impact on different aspects of child development. Researchers observed hundreds of characteristics of creches over several days, which were then summarized across three dimensions: infrastructure, health and sanitation, and activities and program structure. (Most of the standard observation instruments approximate these dimensions.) They then implemented a test of children's social, physical, and mental development, to see how observed creche quality correlated with children's development (table 2.1). They observed that the quality of the infrastructure had a strong positive association with social and physical development: Attending one of the best creches in terms of infrastructure would advance a child by 3.8 months in her social development and 2.4 months in her physical development, relative to attending one of the worst creches. Alternatively, activities and program structure in the best creches added over 3 months to children's social and mental development. Thus, high-quality creches can contribute to children's development across the range of cognitive areas.

Table 2.1: Impact of creche quality on months of child development, measured in months of child development

		Dimensions of development				Statistical significance
		Overall	Social	Physical	Mental	
Dimensions of quality	Overall	1.2	2.3	0.3	1.8	99%
	Infrastructure	–0.9	3.8	2.4	1.2	95%
	Health & sanitation	–1.7	–2.8	–3.0	–2.9	90%
	Activities & program structure	2.5	3.2	–0.04	3.1	Insignificant
	Human resources	1.7	–0.7	2.0	1.2	
	Parents & community relations	–0.2	–0.9	–0.6	–0.5	

Source: Barros et al. (2011a).
Note: Shades of gray refer to statistical significance (white is insignificant). Darker shades refer to more highly significant correlations.

Infrastructure quality

In Brazil, the quality of facilities for early child education is on the rise. High-quality infrastructure can expand learning and interaction opportunities, minimize distractions and wasted time, and make parents feel more comfortable entrusting their children's care to another. Average infrastructure quality improved between 2001 and 2009 in all regions and for both creches and pre-schools. In figure 2.1, infrastructure quality is measured by an index that averages seven quality indicators, available in the census of all registered pre-schools and creches. These measures are the fraction of institutions with a dedicated school building (as opposed to being located in a church, teacher's home, or another place), an indoor bathroom, electricity, a connection to the public water network, a connection to the public sewer network, a library, and a computer. In addition to improving on the overall quality index during 2001–2009, creches in each region improved on nearly every one of the seven individual quality measures.[1] For example, the likelihood of being in a dedicated school building rose from 83 percent to 91 percent, the likelihood of having an indoor bathroom rose from 90 percent to 95 percent, and the likelihood of having a computer rose from 35 percent to 68 percent. The gains, however, have not been evenly distributed across regions of the country.

Pre-school infrastructure in the North deteriorated in some respects over 2001–2009.[2] Pre-schools there became more likely to have a dedicated school building, electricity and a computer. But they became less likely to be connected to the public water or sewer networks, or to have a library. The North saw a 51 percent increase in the total number of registered pre-schools between 2001 and 2009; this rapid expansion might explain drops in some infrastructure quality indicators. Existing data make it impossible to determine whether pre-schools with low-quality infrastructure already existed but were not registered in 2001 (but then had registered by 2009), or whether pre-schools built in the North between 2001 and 2009 had lower-quality infrastructure than did pre-schools already in place in 2001. The inability to distinguish between these stories underscores the importance of registering schools.

ECE infrastructure quality in the North and in the Northeast has consistently lagged behind that of other regions, both in the overall index and in the individual factors included. For example, in 2009 the average infrastructure quality index score of pre-schools

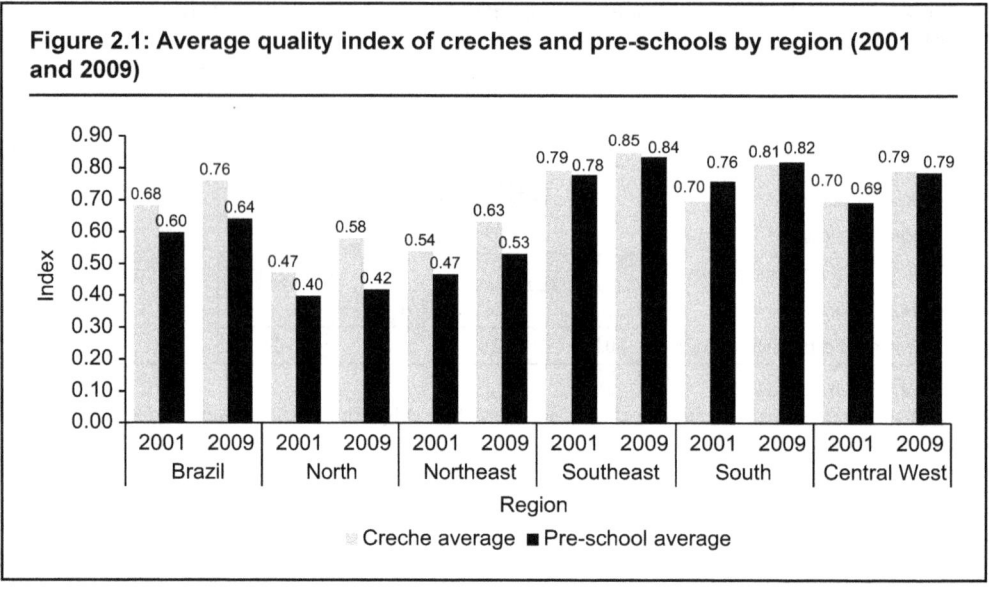

Figure 2.1: Average quality index of creches and pre-schools by region (2001 and 2009)

Source: Censo Escolar (2001, 2009).

in the North was only half that of pre-schools in the Southeast. And while all registered pre-schools and creches in the Southeast and in the South had electricity in 2009, only 75 percent of pre-schools in the North had electricity.

In all regions but the South, creches have higher-quality infrastructure than do pre-schools. Part of this difference may come from the fact that creches are more likely to be private than are pre-schools. In 2009, 43 percent of creches were private, but only 24 percent of pre-schools were private. If parents pay for private schools because they want higher quality infrastructure than is available in public schools, this could explain part of the infrastructure quality differential between creches and pre-schools.[3]

Changes in the number of students per room shed light on whether new enrollments are accommodated through an expansion in the supply of schools or through more intensive use of existing schools. Program quality may decline with class size. While total enrollment has increased, the number of students per classroom has decreased.[4] In pre-schools, class size has decreased from 39 students per classroom to 32 students. Creche class size has remained constant at 26 students per classroom (Evans and Kosec 2011). However, this compares unfavorably with recommendations from the United States' National Association for the Education of Young Children that even five-year-olds have a maximum of ten children per caregiver, and that younger children have lower ratios (NAEYC 2008).

The number of students per classroom remained the same or shrank in every region and for both levels of ECE during 2001–2009 (figure 2.2). The number of classrooms seems to be growing at least as fast as the student population. Regional disparities are again apparent, with the North and the Northeast having the largest number of students per classroom, and the South and the Southeast having the smallest. But these regional disparities in student-room ratios are shrinking over time.

Public creches and pre-schools tend to be of much lower quality than their private counterparts (figure 2.3). Interestingly, contracted (or *conveniada*) private schools tend

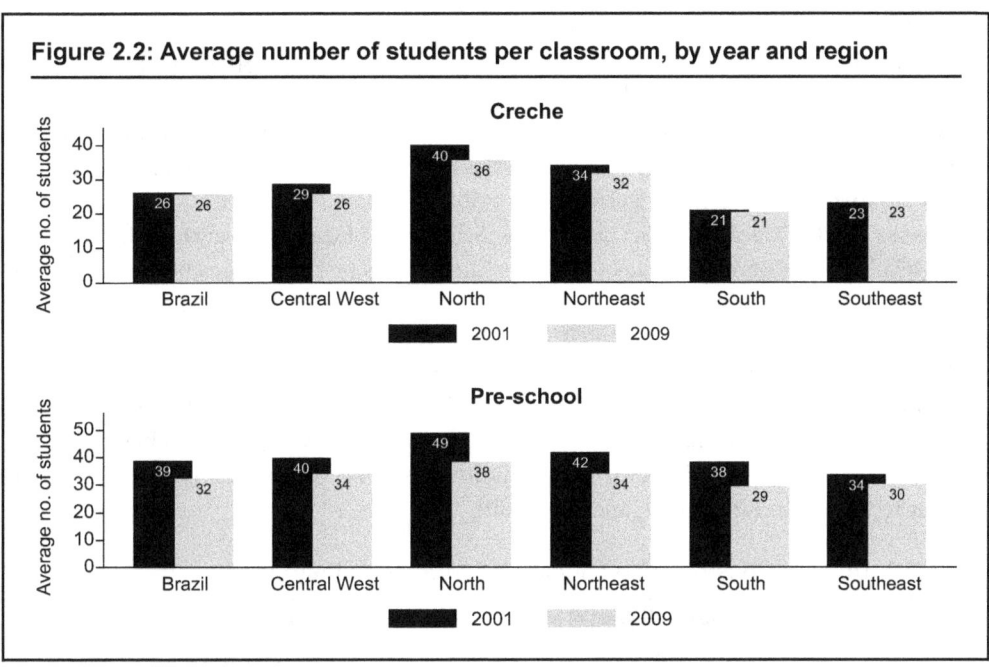

Figure 2.2: Average number of students per classroom, by year and region

Source: Censo Escolar (2001, 2009).

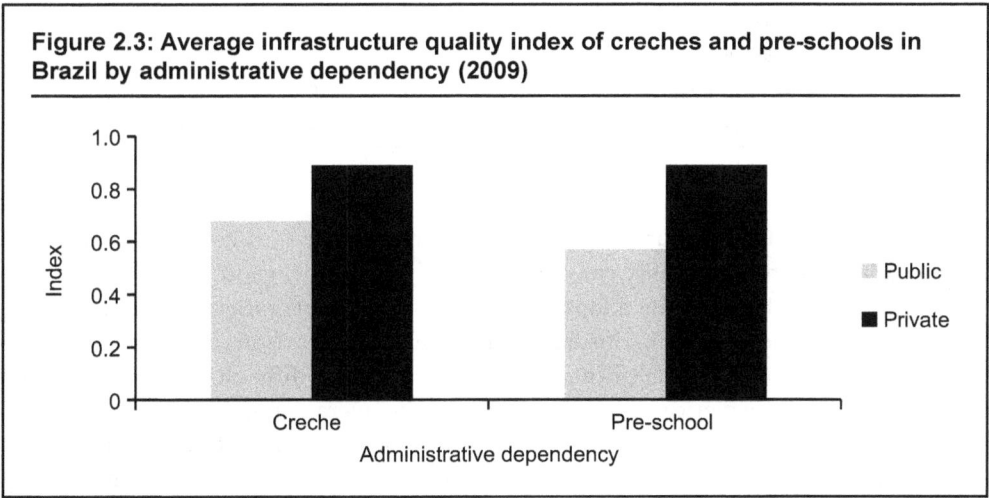

Figure 2.3: Average infrastructure quality index of creches and pre-schools in Brazil by administrative dependency (2009)

Source: Censo Escolar (2001, 2009).

to have infrastructure quality that is higher than that of public schools. This is contrary to the perception in many municipalities, and may reflect a greater concentration of contracted schools in municipalities where the overall creche and pre-school quality is higher. In 2009, the infrastructure quality index of public creches in Brazil was about three-quarters that of private creches, and the quality index of public pre-schools was less than two-thirds that of private pre-schools.

Activities and program quality

While quality infrastructure has proven impacts on children's physical development, it is insufficient to provide children with the cognitive development they need from an early child education center. This is central to Minister of Education Fernando Haddad's statement that, "It is necessary to change the environment of the creche and the pre-school, to fortify these centers as learning establishments" (Weber 2011).

Last year, Fundação Carlos Chagas, the Ministry of Education, and the Inter-American Development Bank collaborated on a study of creches and pre-schools in six capital cities in Brazil: Belém, Campo Grande, Florianópolis, Fortaleza, Rio de Janeiro, and Teresina (Fundação Carlos Chagas 2010). This study employed two of the most standard observational instruments for early child education: the Early Childhood Environment Rating Scale—Revised for pre-schools (ECERS-R, Harms, Clifford and Cryer 2005) and the Infant and Toddler Environment Rating Scale—Revised for creches (ITERS-R, Harms, Cryer and Clifford 2006). The domains of quality measured (see table 2.2) are similar to those used in Rio de Janeiro in 2001.

Table 2.2: Domains in early child education observation instruments

ITERS-R (for centers of children 0–2½ years of age)	ECERS-R (for centers of children 2–5 years of age)
Space and Furnishings	Space and Furnishings
Personal Care Routines	Personal Care Routines
Listening and Talking	Language-Reasoning
Activities	Activities
Interactions	Interactions
Program Structure	Program Structure
Parents and Staff	Parents and Staff

Source: FPG Child Development Institute (n.d.).

The standard ITERS-R and ECERS-R instruments rate ECE centers—overall and in each domain—in four quality categories: inadequate, basic, good, and excellent. The Fundação Carlos Chagas study adapted the scale into five categories: inadequate, basic, adequate, good, and excellent. This adaptation makes comparisons between the Brazilian results and international applications of the instruments difficult. However, a recent study of almost 700 American pre-schools placed the average pre-school evenly within the "adequate" category (LoCasale-Crouch et al. 2007), as did a study of pre-schools in Germany and in Portugal (Tietze et al. 1998).[5] Quality in Brazilian ECE seems significantly lower: Brazilian pre-schools rated "inadequate" in two cities, "basic" in three cities, and "adequate" in just one city. Brazilian creches in two cities rated "basic" on average, whereas creches in the other four cities were "inadequate."[6] Even this measure of quality is troubling, and quality is likely to be even lower in rural areas with access to fewer resources.

Across areas, the study found that—for both creches and pre-schools—the most lacking areas are activities and program structure (figure 2.4). At both age levels, the low quality ratings are largely driven by a lack of good activities, inadequate program structure, and non-stimulating space and furnishings. Within activities, there are deficiencies across the board: in every area from playing with blocks, to physical activities, fine mo-

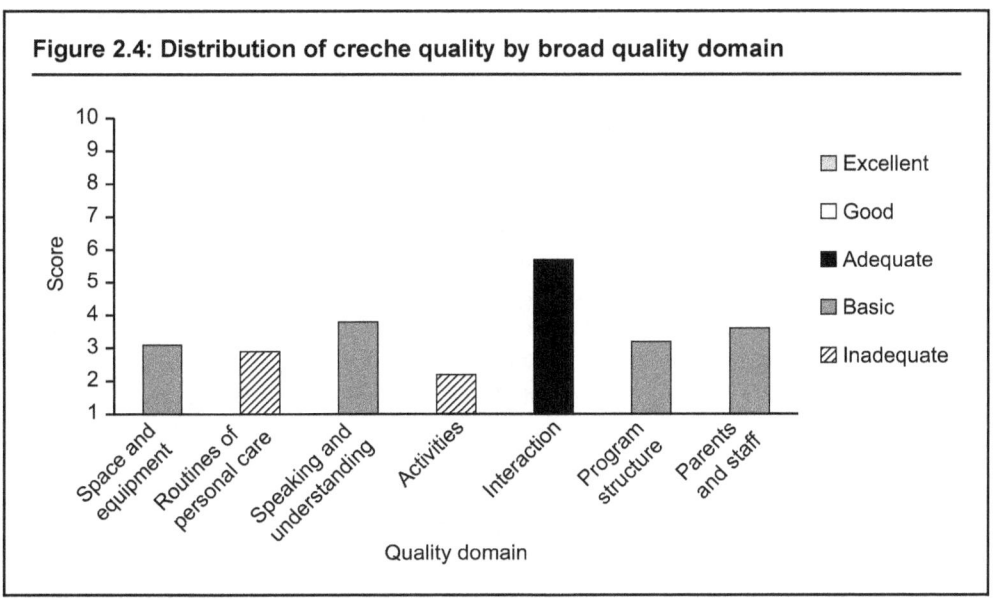

Figure 2.4: Distribution of creche quality by broad quality domain

Source: Fundação Carlos Chagas (2010).
Note: The distribution of scores is very similar for pre-schools. Creches are rated on a scale of 1–10, with 1–3 characterized as inadequate, 3–5 as basic, 5–7 as adequate, 7–8.5 as good, and 8.5–10 as excellent.

tor activities (puzzles, games, etc.), nature or science activities, use of books, etc. (figure 2.5). The creche level, for example, lacks activities involving books, those incorporating music and movement, nature and science activities, and appropriate use of videos and computers (i.e., age-appropriate content, for appropriate periods of time, and only for children over 12 months of age).

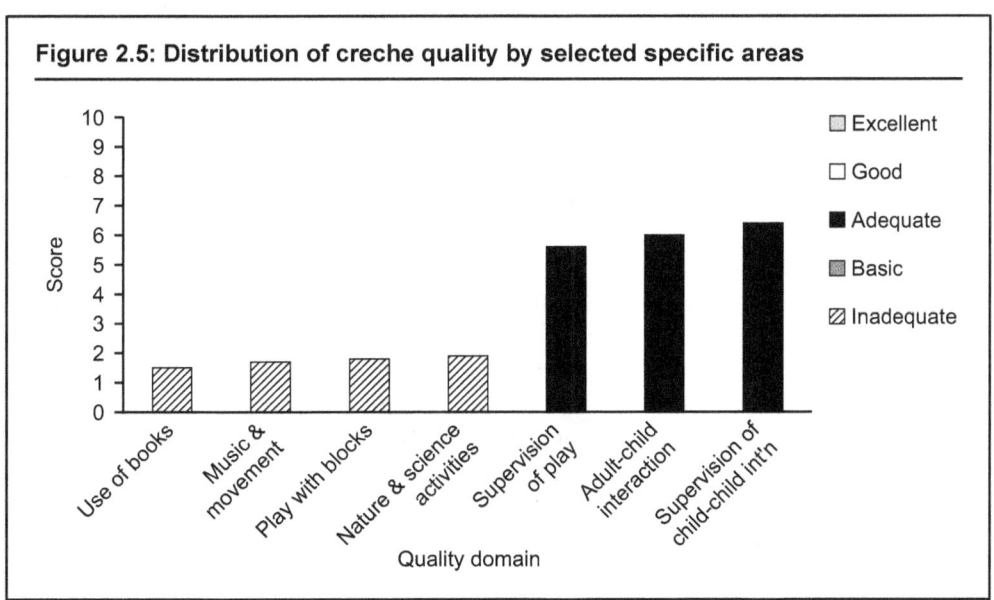

Figure 2.5: Distribution of creche quality by selected specific areas

Source: Fundação Carlos Chagas (2010).

On the other hand, the strongest area for both creches and pre-schools is interactions. Within that area, interactions between caregivers and children are rated relatively highly. That said, interactions are still rated as "adequate," failing to achieve either "good" or "excellent" status. Still, this suggests that caregivers are engaged with children, and mostly need help involving those children in constructive activities.

These averages suggest particularly bad conditions for some of the worst creches and pre-schools. In fact, half of creches and almost one-third of pre-schools were found to be "inadequate" whereas only 1 percent of creches and 4 percent of pre-schools achieved a "good" rating (figure 2.6). Not a single institution achieved an "excellent" rating. Likewise, the previously-discussed 2001 study of 100 creches in Rio de Janeiro found major quality gaps between the best and worst creches. The size of these gaps is striking: The best fifth of creches were rated two and a half times better in activities and program structure than were the worst fifth of creches (Barros et al. 2011a).

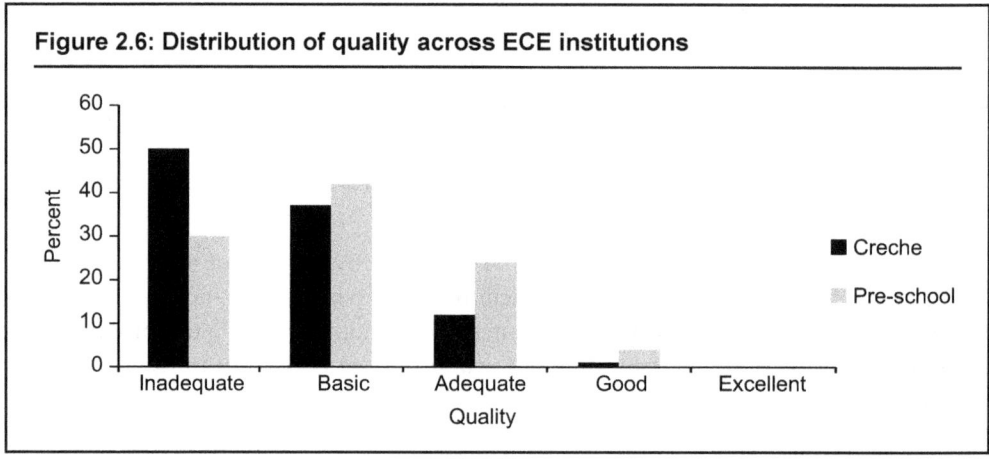

Source: Fundação Carlos Chagas (2010).

The Fundação Carlos Chagas study did not find any systematic difference in observed quality across private, public, or *conveniado* schools. However, Early Child Development Spaces (EDIs)[7]—or educational institutions with only creche and/or pre-school—tended to be of significantly higher quality than those connected to a primary school.[8]

What about teachers?

Measuring the quality of teaching is difficult, and the current best measures applied to higher levels of education rely on student test scores. This is impossible at the level of early child education, where universal student testing is nonexistent and measurement of child outcomes may be much less exact. In primary education, the teacher has been identified as the single most important factor for student success (Hanushek and Rivkin 2010). Yet while teachers have an essential influence on children, years of teacher education does not seem to matter much for student outcomes; a survey of 170 different studies examining the relationship between teacher education and student outcomes found that 91 percent of them found either no relationship or—in a few cases—even a negative relationship. Among the best studies in terms of methodology, none found a positive relationship between teacher education and student outcomes (Hanushek and Rivkin

2004). Thus, teacher quality is clearly important, but a teacher's formal educational level is a poor proxy for actual effectiveness.

Dozens of studies have explored the relationship between caregiver education and observed center quality at the ECE level (Barnett 2003 and Whitebook 2003), and many have found a positive correlation. However, many of these studies fail to control for other characteristics that are likely correlated with teacher education, such as the wealth of the community, which could both attract more educated teachers and have other characteristics that would suggest better observed quality.

A recent study overcomes some of those failings by examining seven major preschool programs in the United States using the same method and including a broad range of control variables (Early et al. 2007). They examined the relationship between teacher education and four different outcomes: classroom quality, receptive vocabulary (i.e., the words one understands well enough to recognize when read or heard), pre-reading skills, and early math skills. When the researchers examined whether the highest degree attained by the lead teachers could predict these outcomes, there was evidence of a positive relationship in only six out of 27 different analyses.[9] When the researchers focused on the highest education levels among teachers with a major in ECE, the results were once again weak: only two out of 19 analyses showed evidence of a positive association. Finally, the researchers looked specifically at teachers with a Bachelor's degree, to see whether a major in ECE had a significant impact in that case: exactly one of 23 analyses showed a significant positive relationship.

In other words, a careful, consistent examination across seven different large-scale studies showed no consistent relationship between teacher education and student performance. Does that mean that teacher or caregiver education does not matter? Rather, the lack of a relationship implies that broad measures of teacher education, even with a specialization in ECE, do not predict outcomes. Most likely, this implies that current programs of teacher education in the United States do not—on average—equip teachers with the skills needed to effectively improve children's cognitive development.

Furthermore, teachers of early child education in Brazil have significantly less education than do primary and lower secondary school teachers (figure 2.7). There may be some

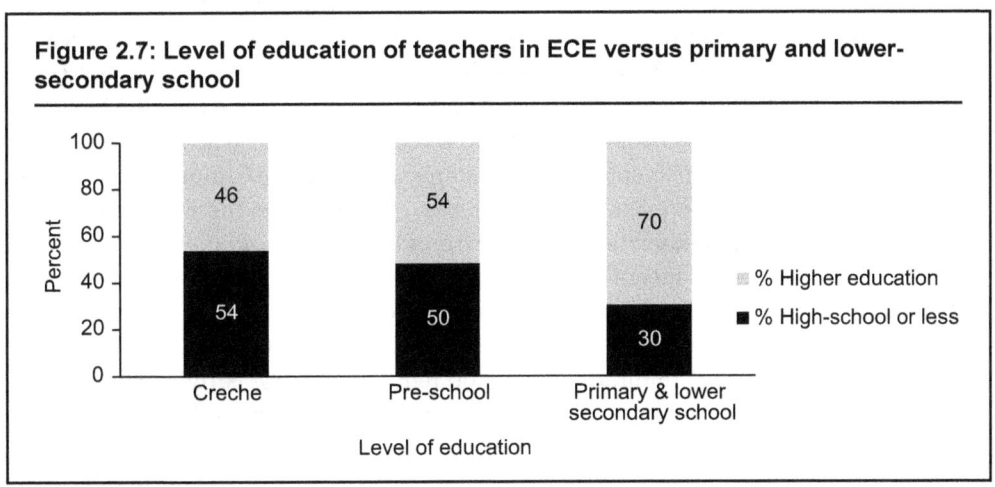

Figure 2.7: Level of education of teachers in ECE versus primary and lower-secondary school

Source: Censo Escolar, "Sinopse do Professor," 2009.

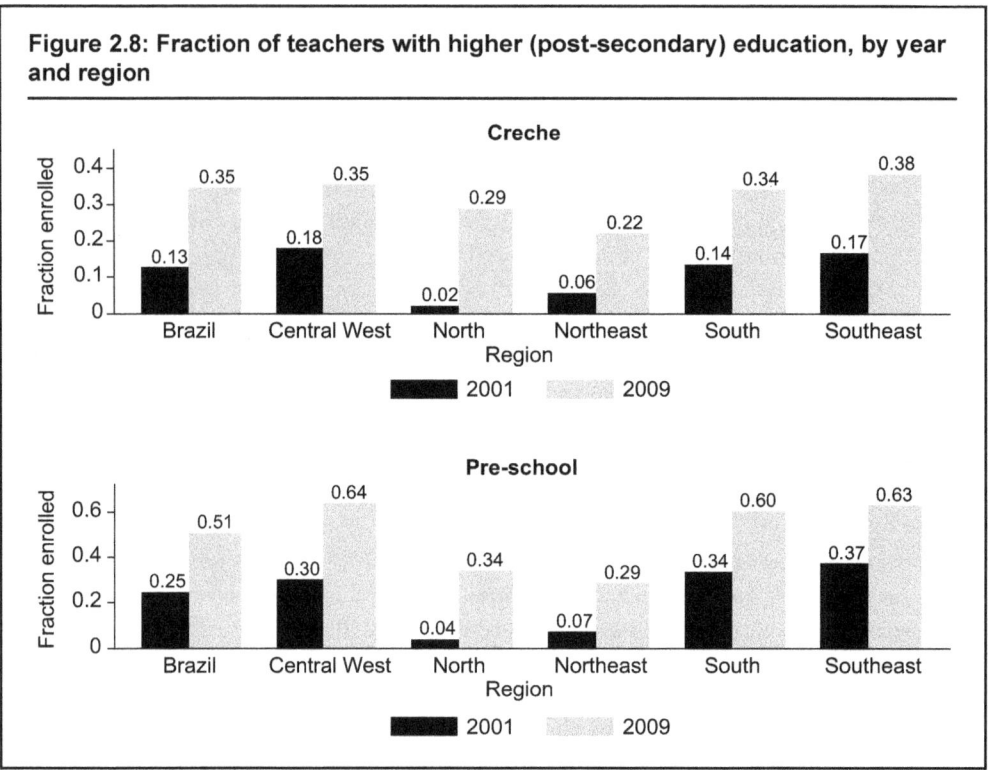

Figure 2.8: Fraction of teachers with higher (post-secondary) education, by year and region

Source: Censo Escolar (2001, 2009).

threshold below which teachers are simply ineffective. This report does not rule out the importance of a minimum standard of teacher education. For example, the recent Brazilian requirements that Brazilian teachers have secondary education should ensure literacy and better capacity for teachers to take advantage of other resources and materials. It may also raise the prestige of the profession, attracting more competent individuals.

The qualifications of ECE teachers have—as in infrastructure—improved dramatically over time, with the proportion of teachers with some post-secondary education more than doubling from 2001 to 2009 in both creches and pre-schools (figure 2.8). Between 2001 and 2009, the fraction of pre-school teachers with higher education increased by 70 percent or more in all regions, and the fraction of creche teachers with higher education increased by 94 percent or more in all regions. Regional differences in teacher education also became less pronounced over this period. While the top region had a pre-school teacher higher education rate nine times that of the bottom region in 2001, it had just over two times the rate of the lowest-performing region in 2009. Creche teachers showed a similar pattern. If surpassing a minimum level of teacher education is important for improved child outcomes, then these trends bode well across the country. Most comparator countries have minimum education requirements for early child education providers, usually a university degree for pre-school teachers and at least a secondary school degree for creche providers (table 2.3).

Table 2.3: Teacher qualifications required in Brazil and comparator countries

Country	Teacher qualifications
Brazil	Teachers in creches and pre-school • Completion of secondary school
Chile	Teachers and directors: • Five-year university degree in pre-school education Professional technicians (for 2–4 and 4–6 age groups): • Two-year post-secondary pre-school technician degree Educator assistants: • No mandatory professional qualifications
Mexico (creche)	Formal center teachers: • University degree in child development Parent education promoters (in CONAFE, the program designed for rural and vulnerable areas): • Secondary school completion and CONAFE training
Mexico (pre-school)	General and indigenous pre-school teachers: • University degree in child development CONAFE community school instructors: • Secondary school completion and CONAFE training
New Zealand	Educators in teacher-led services: • 3-year Diploma in Teaching for early childhood education Educators in parent-led services: • No mandatory professional qualifications
Sweden	Pre-school teachers: • 3.5-year university degree in teaching Child assistants: • Upper secondary professional diploma Family day care workers: • No mandatory professional qualifications

Source: Brazil: Decree 6.755 (29 January 2009). Other countries: Bruns et al. (2010).

The National Network for Early Childhood already calls for the completion of three ambitious goals over the next decade: (a) in ten years, all directors of ECE institutions will have higher education, (b) in six years, all teachers will have ECD training at the higher education level, and (c) in ten years, all teachers will have training in inclusive education and in Brazilian sign language (for the deaf). The goal that each ECD provider has substantial training in ECD specifically (beyond short distance courses) is an excellent one. However, achieving it in the next six years is likely to be a true challenge as many ECD caregivers currently lack that training; to date, ECD-specific training has been offered at only a very limited level in Brazil.

Key areas to improve in quality

Improving early child education quality means improving both program structure and program activities. This is consistent with findings from other countries: A major study of the quality of pre-schools in the United Kingdom found activities to be one of the weakest areas despite strong interpersonal interactions, echoing the Brazil study (Sylva et al. 2004). A study of creches in the United States found weaknesses in the same kinds of activities and in children's opportunities to interact with books, as did a study on Brazil (Cryer and Burchinal 1997). Yet the finding that interactions are strong in Brazilian pre-schools and creches suggests that educators want to provide quality services, and are simply lacking the knowledge and resources to provide high-quality structure and activities.

Monitoring and supervision by the government could directly help centers improve their program structure and activities. An effective system of knowledge-sharing and the provision of information about best practice would equip centers with the tools necessary to invest in the right types of quality.

The role of parents in monitoring quality

Unfortunately, parents have trouble objectively judging the quality of early child education centers, thus highlighting the importance of the government's role as overseer. A 2001 study of creches in Rio de Janeiro asked parents about their perceptions of their children's creches and showed that parents thought almost all creches were of high quality (figure 2.9), completely independent of the actual quality, which was measured separately using an objective rating tool (Barros et al. 2011a). This confirms similar findings in studies of parent perceptions of pre-schools in Germany and in the United States (Cryer, Tietze and Wessels 2002), as well as a finding that parents vastly overestimate the amount of regulation the government provides for child care centers in the United States (NACCRRA 2009). Parents' perceptions of child care center quality tend to be particularly misguided when it comes to elements that are not easily monitored, such as activities and supervision, as opposed to elements that are more easily observed such as the physical space (Cryer and Burchinal 1997). Because parents do not have sufficient information to evaluate centers well on exactly the areas—such as activities and program structure—where Brazilian creches and pre-schools need major improvements, there is an argument for federal and municipal governments to step in to assist in measuring and evaluating quality.

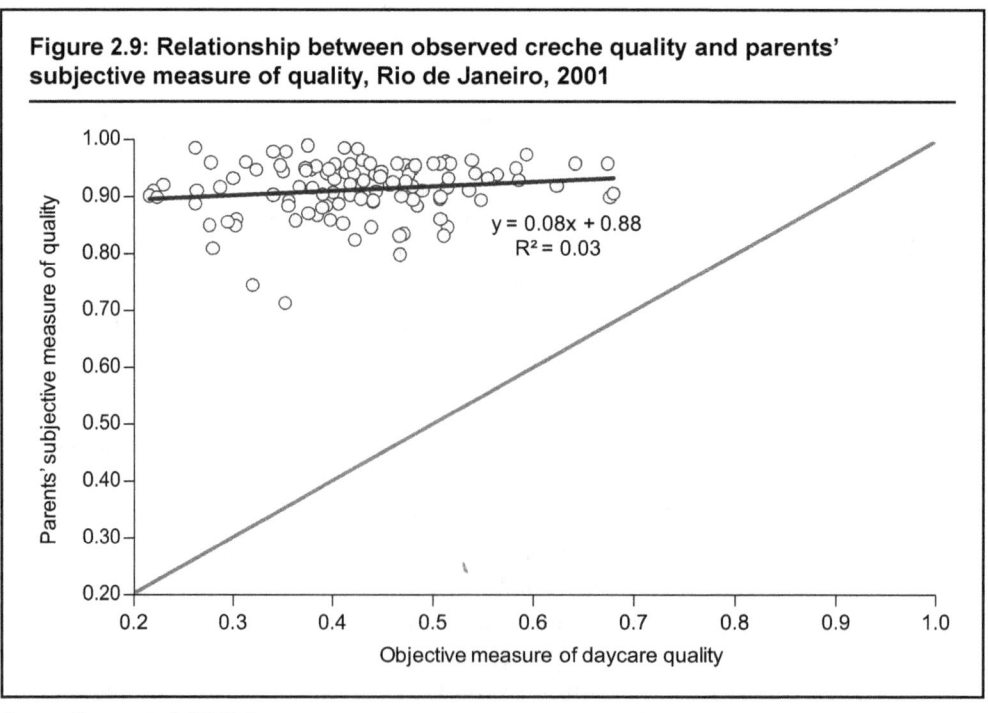

Figure 2.9: Relationship between observed creche quality and parents' subjective measure of quality, Rio de Janeiro, 2001

$y = 0.08x + 0.88$
$R^2 = 0.03$

Source: Barros et al. (2011a).

Curricular and Program Structure Improvement

Two of the most widely-touted high-return early child education programs are the Perry Pre-school and the Abecedarian programs, and each of those programs had a high-quality curriculum that guided the activities of caregivers and children. A randomized trial in the United States compared three curricular models for three and four-year-olds; the results showed far better long-term life outcomes for children with curricula in which children initiated activities and teachers then responded or in which teachers and children planned activities together, as compared to a more scripted curriculum (Schweinhart and Weikart 1998). This is very different from most primary school curricula, so it is not surprising if a standard education training program would be insufficient to effectively prepare ECE providers.

In Brazil, the Ministry of Education published a three volume curricular guide in 1988 which has rich information on how to design activities for early child education centers. Further, the National Education Council published a set of guiding directives for ECE curricular proposals in 2009.[10] A valuable next step would be to provide practical workbooks or guides with lesson plans containing specific activities in pre-reading, pre-mathematics, and other areas, to help educators not only understand what activities are effective, but also how to implement them. In order to shift to more child-directed activities, ECE educators will need improved, specific training in this kind of open curriculum, as well as sufficiently small groups of children such that each child can initiate activities.

Municipalities can of course take the initiative to supplement the Ministry resources. The Municipality of Rio de Janeiro has developed its own curricular guidelines with specific suggestions of activities to develop key skills. The Rio guidelines also provide guidance on program structure, giving priority to cognitive activities in the mornings, followed by reading activities in the early afternoon, and fresh air activities later. The guides suggest how a day could be structured, alternating these activities with free play (Barros et al. 2010). The next step will be shifting to a more child-directed program structure. Greater communication between municipalities might help them to leverage one another's experiences with effective curricular guides and program structures.

Monitoring Program Quality

Many countries have implemented programs to strengthen monitoring of quality for early child development (see box 2.1). The federal government in the United States has proposed new legislation to evaluate each of the nation's Head Start programs over the next three years, examining program performance using an established classroom observation rating instrument, as well as fiscal integrity and licensing standards. Each year, the bottom 25 percent of Head Start programs will compete with private centers for government funding (Haskins and Barnett 2010, US Department of Health & Human Services 2010). This competition will create incentives for program directors to perform and will reduce the persistence of ineffective programs. Likewise in Sweden, all child care centers must be registered and undergo annual reviews, including supervision, in order to continue functioning (OECD 2006).

> **Box 2.1: Impact evaluation for early child development**
>
> Much of the global knowledge on the importance of early child education stems from a few rigorous impact evaluations of child development programs. The High/Scope Perry Pre-school Study and the Abecedarian program both took advantage of the fact that they were not universal programs—in fact, they were both small pilots—to randomly assign the program among those children most in need, to allow comparisons over time between those who participated and those who did not.
>
> Evidence of comparable quality in Latin America is very limited. Most of Brazil's evidence on Early Child Education comes from comparisons in later schooling outcomes between children who attended creches or pre-schools and those who did not, which yields some insight but also leaves open the possibility that other factors may be affecting these outcomes. For example, parents who value schooling may be more likely to enroll a child in pre-school and their child may also have strong long-term school outcomes, but the latter could be due to the parent spending time helping the child learn, something not captured in the comparison of pre-schoolers and non-pre-schoolers.
>
> The Municipality of Rio de Janeiro has—like the Perry Pre-school program—taken advantage of non-universal coverage to use a lottery to assign scarce slots among the neediest of children. This allows for comparisons among comparable children who received public creche care and those who did not. The study began in 2007. Early results show significant impacts on mothers' labor force participation, and results on children's cognitive development will be collected in 2011.
>
> This study and more like it in the future will strengthen the evidence base for the best ways to deliver quality early child education in Brazil.

The United States is an interesting comparator for Brazil given the relatively similar size and level of decentralization in the system. At the most basic level of ensuring quality, almost all states in the United States require child care centers and pre-schools (even completely private ones) to be licensed. Licensing usually includes a renewal either once a year or every other year, and most states will shut down child care centers or pre-schools that do not satisfy licensing requirements. However, while licensing generally covers a broad range of areas, including staff age, facilities quality, and training guidelines, meeting these standards is a necessary but far from sufficient condition to achieve quality early child education (NARA 2006).

Likewise, 26 states or localities have implemented Quality Rating Systems (QRS) for child care and ECE centers. These systems rate centers on a wide variety of quality standards, generally including the following: child-staff ratios and group size, staff training and education, and an assessment of the classroom and learning environment (Zellman and Perlman 2008). The full range of quality standards and how ratings tend to be assigned is shown in Appendix D. Most of these ratings systems then provide consequences: inducements for centers to improve, support for centers that are weak, and closure for the direst cases. These programs are voluntary in most cases, yet many centers participate because of the variety of incentives provided. State and local governments also hope that, as more centers participate, parents will use the ratings to choose centers. Thus more centers will have an incentive to join, since a non-rating will be interpreted as a poor rating. In addition, two-thirds of these QRS have built in an evaluation of the rating system itself. These evaluations show systematic improvements in the quality of

Early Child Education centers, as measured by observational instruments, after participating in a QRS (Tout et al. 2010).[11]

Environmental rating scales

Almost all of the QRSs in the United States have employed some sort of observational measure (Tout et al. 2010). Most have used the ITERS-R for childcare centers and the ECERS-R for pre-schools. The instrument currently proposed by the United States Department of Health and Human Services for use to evaluate Head Start programs is the Classroom Assessment Scoring System (CLASS), which is designed for pre-school and the first few years of elementary school (La Paro, Pianta and Stuhlman 2004).[12]

Versions of several of these instruments have been implemented in Brazil. In 2009, Fundação Carlos Chagas adapted the ECERS-R and ITERS-R for Brazil and applied them in creches and pre-schools in six capital municipalities, with the results earlier in this chapter (Fundação Carlos Chagas 2010).[13] In addition, IPEA in 2001 applied an instrument which evaluates similar areas to the ECERS-R in a study of 100 pre-schools in Rio de Janeiro, as presented at the beginning of this chapter (Barros et al. 2011a). The Municipality of Rio de Janeiro is currently designing a quality monitoring system that will use the Brazilian adaptations of ITERS-R and ECERS-R across its creches and pre-schools, with a similar purpose as the QRS programs in the United States (Barros et al. 2010).

Child development measurements

Testing children's cognitive and socio-emotional development can play an important role in gauging the overall health of the ECE system as well as identifying children with special needs. Of course, test results at any age must be safeguarded to prevent abuse. As the consequences of an assessment increase in importance, so does the importance of using high-quality instruments implemented by well-trained examiners. For example, a simple child monitoring test can have implications for how a child's family views the potential of that child. Other tests, used to screen for whether a child requires special services, can directly affect a long-term education trajectory. It is therefore essential to ensure that tests are implemented appropriately and that the results are used with care (Snow and Van Hemel 2008). This is in line with the National Education Council's 2009 judgment proposing that ECE evaluations not be used to hold back individual students.[14]

If the goal is to gauge the quality of the system, then testing a sample of students in the system can be sufficient and cost-effective. The test results can be delinked from child-specific identifiers to protect children's well-being. At the same time, many QRSs in the United States require child care centers to provide screenings to ensure that children are developing appropriately and to see if they need any additional services. In no case are these assessments linked to the center's incentives: They are purely intended to raise the quality of services for the child. Most programs that require assessments, however, must provide evidence that information from the assessment is used for individual planning for the children, and must share the information with parents, as in the New Mexico (United States) program (Look for the Stars 2005).

A variety of instruments are in use in U.S. QRSs,[15] but the recommended instruments tend to have two characteristics in common: (1) Most of them are designed as screening tools, rather than broad measures of child development, and (2) all of them rely on ratings and reports from parents or child care providers, rather than direct assessment with children. One that is frequently used is the Ages and Stages questionnaire, which has recently been translated and validated for use in the municipality of Rio de Janeiro (Carvalho et al. 2011).

This testing can guide municipalities to improve. Researchers in Rio de Janeiro recently applied the Ages and Stages questionnaire to all present students in 500 creches, then compared cognitive and motor development for students in the first year to that of students in the last year. This provided an estimate of the value-added of a creche.[16] The municipality will now visit the creches with highest value added and seek to learn what they are doing right, to share that with the rest of the network (Barros et al. 2011c). More systematic knowledge sharing within and across early child education systems is a critically important way in which Brazil could identify areas for improvement.

Interventions to support improvements

While most of the QRSs in the United States are voluntary, one of the reasons to participate is that all participating creches and pre-schools receive access to training, most often in the following areas: (1) assessment of the environment, (2) language and literacy, (3) specific curriculum training, (4) business practices, (5) safety, (6) social and emotional development, and (7) child assessments (Tout et al. 2010).

A number of programs, both in the United States and abroad, offer improvement grants targeted to some element of pre-school quality. Some aim to improve the quality of teachers with general grants to early child educators to earn higher degrees, in Jamaica, Australia (Victoria) and the United States (New York City). Given the tenuous link between general teacher qualifications and student performance, this approach may have limited effectiveness unless it is restricted to high quality trainings. Another approach, seeking to link teacher training more closely with desired outcomes, is the Maine Roads to Quality Registry (United States), in which early child educators join a program that provides career counseling, eligibility for scholarships, and a 180-hour training program closely-aligned with the state's identified learning goals (Howes et al. 2008).

Improving Quality through Improved Incentives

At the level of primary education, education systems around the world are exploring various ways to reward performance by monitoring student outcomes and rewarding teachers and schools that demonstrate improvements. There has been promising evidence on these programs, showing that incentives for teachers and schools have major impacts—in India, for example (Muralidharan and Sundararaman 2009)—but also evidence to the contrary, showing no effects—in a recent program in the United States (Springer et al. 2010).

More than fifteen states and municipalities across Brazil have implemented pay-for-performance programs, linking student improvements to monetary bonuses for teachers. At the level of early child education, how can one encourage teachers to focus on activities that will be most helpful to their young students in preparing them for the next phase of their education?

A number of programs in the United States have established incentive programs for pre-school and child care facilities. These programs are not linked to direct child development measurements, but rather to systems that monitor quality through observation. The awards can be linked to a particular quality improvement plan, or in some cases the centers are free to use them as they wish (Tout et al. 2010).

Improving Quality through Improved In-Service Training and Supervision

As in later years of education, the provider or teacher is likely the most important factor in determining the success or failure of a child's early education experience. Two essential components of ensuring high quality care and teaching are the training and supervision of early child educators. Many municipalities in Brazil are seeking to improve in these areas. Box 2.2 includes two examples.

Box 2.2: Training and supervision in two municipalities

The municipality of Araraquara (in São Paulo) is improving the continuing education of its early child educators, and São Bernardo do Campo (also in São Paulo) is strengthening its program of school supervision. Araraquara has experimented with both internal training (of early child educators by the school director) and external training (by a municipal team). While internal training has shown certain strengths in terms of the directors' familiarity with the school and the teachers, encouraging directors to take responsibility for this has proved challenging (Bomfim, Ferreira, and Oliveira 2011). In São Bernardo do Campo, the program has struggled with defining the precise role of the supervisor to maximize effectiveness. This process of experimentation and revision is reflective of what many municipalities across Brazil experience. In both cases, the federal government also plays a role in developing materials to guide these processes, but much is left to the municipalities (Ferreira, Oliveira, and Bomfim 2011).

As discussed earlier, simple levels of training do not predict success in early child education. Teachers need training, but in particular, they need training in hands-on activities and interactions to foster child cognitive development. A study of the highly effective Perry Pre-school program in the United States indicates that key elements of the program's success were (1) systematic *in-service* training in early child development and education (general education training was found to be unhelpful as the form of pedagogy is distinctive in early childhood), and (2) *ongoing supervision* by supervisors who are experts in the curriculum (Schweinhart, Barnes, and Weikhart 2005).

Brazil currently has several in-service training programs for early child educators. A federal program entitled Proinfantil provides distance training to teachers in creches and pre-schools; its goal is to train 23,000 educators by July 2011. The Proinfantil curriculum has six key areas: four content areas—(1) language, (2) identity, society, and culture, (3) mathematics and logic, (4) life and nature—and two methodological areas— (5) foundations of education and (6) organization of teaching. This program is a start to supplying ECE providers with the building blocks they need, but teachers still need more hands-on training. Nonprofit initiatives have sprouted to fill the demand, such as the Education Tables (*Mesas Educadores*) from the Millennium Fund for Early Childhood, which are resource centers providing training for in-service early child development providers. Likewise, five nonprofits have joined to support *Formar em Rede*, which provides distance learning to early child educators in close to fifty municipalities around Brazil. More general in-service programs with strong hands-on training in preparing high-quality activities to improve cognitive development are lacking.

Improving Quality through Knowledge Sharing

Because early child education programs are the responsibility of the municipal education secretaries, and because Brazil has over 5,500 municipalities, the variation in programs is extensive. State governments have no formal role in early child education, although occasionally they will support municipalities, as in Acre's Asas da Florestania Infantil program and in Rio Grande do Sul's Primeira Infância Melhor program, which is health-based but includes child cognitive stimulation. The federal government also has programs to support municipal efforts. Finally, the non-government sector is actively involved in early child education.

Federal role

Despite federal funding channeled to municipalities for recurrent costs of early child education through FUNDEB, most municipalities have insufficient early child education centers to meet demand. The federal program Pró-Infância provides funding to municipalities to address this insufficiency; it has so far funded over 2,000 centers, and provided resources to equip several hundred more. A second major federal program, Proinfantil, that provides training, was discussed in the previous section. The federal government consistently sponsors and publishes guidance for municipalities on a range of topics, including how to develop contracts with nonprofit ECE providers, indicators of quality in ECE, curricular references, and others.[17] Creches and pre-schools are also included in some more general programs, such as the National School Library Program, which selects and provides books for educational institutions of all levels (MEC 2009).

Municipal programs have the opportunity to inform others

Many municipalities are investing in their early child education programs, developing specialized curricula, monitoring systems, improved training for caregivers, and more. With over 5,000 municipalities across Brazil, there is great opportunity for these municipalities to learn from each other.

Some public programs target specific areas, and their curricula may be of interest to other municipalities. For example, the Municipality of Santarém (State of Pará) has developed the program Eco-Schools (Santarém 2010), which provides lessons about the environment beginning in ECE. The Municipality of Campinas (State of São Paulo) has developed Prodança-Criança Escola to teach children dance in order to provide a range of development opportunities. Likewise, the Municipality of Rio de Janeiro has developed a curriculum of 40 lessons to provide training to parents of creche children. These span education, health, and social assistance (see the curriculum outline in Appendix F). The curriculum includes DVDs, workbooks, and discussion guides. Likewise, the program of home-based education visits developed by the state of Acre (described further in the next chapter) includes workbooks and educational agent guides which demonstrate (both to the agents and then to the parents) how to use common objects available near the home as tools of cognitive stimulation. Clearly, these curricula and others like them represent a potential educational resource for other municipalities.

In addition to these curricula, many municipalities have invested in additional innovative programs from which others can learn and adapt. For example, the municipality of Macapá (in Amapá), introduced the program Revivendo as Tradições, whereby local cultural traditions are woven into play and learning activities. Rio de Janeiro is adapting Bookstart, a U.K. program to expose children ages 0–3 to positive reading experiences by providing reading materials and encouragement to parents. Salvador (in Bahia) established Pequeno Cidadão, in which pre-schoolers go to a public office to receive their own identity cards, and are guided through all the necessary steps. They learn the national anthem, hear stories about their rights as citizens, and are invited to share their own relevant experiences. In Lucas do Rio Verde (in Mato Grosso), creche participants take walks to a variety of locations: the supermarket, where they learn about fruits and vegetables, or a local artisan's shop, where they learn about regional art and painting. In Belém (Pará), pre-school children learn math by collecting and counting different kinds of used telephone calling cards, going on to practice reading and learning about the Pará landmarks depicted on the cards.[18] Access to these types of programs, and evidence on which are most successful, will help municipalities to build on the experiences of others.

How can municipalities share information?

Municipalities currently have few tools that they can use to learn from each other's programs. Several networks for early child development exist, including the National Network for Early Childhood. However, this network focuses less on program-level knowledge sharing and more on improving national policy. The National Union of Municipal Education Leaders (UNDIME) likewise disseminates some documents on national early education policy.

Recently, two initiatives for more direct information sharing have been launched. One is the Network for Cooperation and Peace for Children, which is a social networking site (a là Facebook) where policy makers, nonprofit workers, educators, and other interested citizens actively exchange information. The site currently has nearly 500 members. A second initiative launched by the National Forum for Early Child Development and the World Bank, called the Network for Cooperation in Early Child Development, seeks to provide a map of early child development services across Brazil. It also provides a social networking site focused on sharing exactly the kinds of materials described above: information on innovative programs, experiences, and best practices.

The federal government can also play a role in helping municipalities learn from one another. An initiative that the federal government formerly sponsored is an annual Prize for Quality in Early Child Education, which ran from 2000 through 2005 and highlighted innovative projects implemented by individual municipalities or ECE centers.

Lessons

There are a number of ways in which Brazil can contribute to ECE quality improvements in key areas. First, the federal government can develop more specific curricular guides that provide local creches and pre-schools with outlines for activities. Second, Brazil can introduce systematic monitoring by providing access to a standard observational tool. Third, the federal government can set licensing guidelines for minimum standards in quality for municipalities to adapt. This is a step beyond the existing guidelines for the quality of creches: it entails both quality minimums and guidelines for the implementation of a licensing program. Finally, Brazil can encourage more systematic monitoring within municipalities and more fluid knowledge sharing across municipalities.

Notes

1. The only exception is that creches in the Central West saw a one percentage point decline in access to the public sewer network. All other regions improved in every infrastructure category.
2. This is also the region with the farthest to go in terms of achieving universal pre-school access.
3. It is also possible that a more representative sample of pre-schools are registered and thus included in the Census of Schools, whereas only creches with relatively good infrastructure are reg-

istered. This might be the case since pre-school is a higher and more prevalent level of education, and may be more likely to take place in schools that offer primary education (and thus are more closely regulated and monitored).

4. The Census of Schools does not indicate how many rooms are dedicated to each level of education. However, it does indicate how many total rooms and how many total students there are in schools that offer creche-level education, and in schools that offer pre-school-level education. As a result, our indicator of students per room in creches (pre-schools) is total students per room in schools that offer creche- (pre-school-) level education.

5. The Germany and Portugal study uses the ECERS, whereas the United States study uses the ECERS-R (of which the Brazilian study is an adaptation). Comparability of the two instruments has been demonstrated (Sakai et al. 2003).

6. Again, the scales are not exactly the same, so these comparisons should be taken with caution.

7. *Espaços de Desenvolvimento Infantil*, commonly referred to as EDIs

8. It cannot be ruled out that this is because EDIs are newer than other institutions.

9. The 27 analyses are the following: 4 outcomes x 7 studies = 28 analyses, minus one study that did not carry out the reading test.

10. National Education Council Judgment 20/2009 (Parecer CNE/CEB N° 20/2009).

11. Only one study has examined the relationship between QRS participation and changes in *child* outcomes. A study of the United States (Colorado) program showed no relationship, although one-third of creches had dropped out by the end of the study (Zellman et al. 2008).

12. The CLASS instrument examines teacher-student interactions in pre-schools in three domains: emotional support, classroom organization, and instructional support. Each domain is broken down into dimensions such as positive climate (to promote children's enjoyment of the classroom environment) and concept development (to promote higher-order thinking and cognition) (Teachstone 2011).

13. In Portuguese, the scales are entitled *Escala de Avaliação de Ambientes para Bebês e Crianças Pequenas (ESAC)* and *Escala de Avaliação de Ambientes da Educação Infantil* (Barros et al. 2010).

14. Parecer CNE/CEB N° 20/2009.

15. Appendix E provides details on selected instruments.

16. This assumes the absence of cohort effects, in which the average cognitive development of children in Rio born—for example—in 2008 is significantly lower than that of those born in 2010.

17. A list of recent publications is provided in Appendix G.

18. Several of these examples are drawn from Prêmio Qualidade na Educação Infantil 2004.

CHAPTER 3

How to Reach the Very Poorest Children

Access to Early Child Education around the World

Brazil has increased creche enrollment extensively over the past fifteen years. With 18 percent of children ages 0–3 covered, it now exceeds the level in Mexico (for 0–3 years old) and has a comparable level to that of Chile (figure 3.1). However, creche enrollment still lags significantly behind countries with more established programs, such as New Zealand, Sweden, and the OECD as a whole. These gaps reflect policy differences. Chile and Mexico have targeted policies for child care at the earliest ages. Sweden provides full-time care and education in pre-schools from age one (Bruns et al. 2010).

An increasing number of countries are seeking universal pre-school coverage for children ages four and five. Brazil—with 75 percent enrollment for 4–5 year olds—lags behind the OECD average of 85 percent, but has enrollment comparable to that found in Chile (figure 3.2). Among Latin American countries, Brazil and Mexico are the only two that have made pre-school mandatory for children ages four and five. Mexico's experience is especially relevant to Brazil since it, like Brazil, seeks to achieve universal pre-school coverage by 2016. Mexico has achieved almost 100 percent coverage for five-year-olds, and well over 90 percent for four-year-olds. But one result of this rapid expansion in Mexico has been a drop in enrollment for three-year-olds in 2005, as efforts and resources were focused on four- and five-year-olds. The resources provided by Brazil's education fund (FUNDEB) for both creches and pre-schools should help to mitigate that

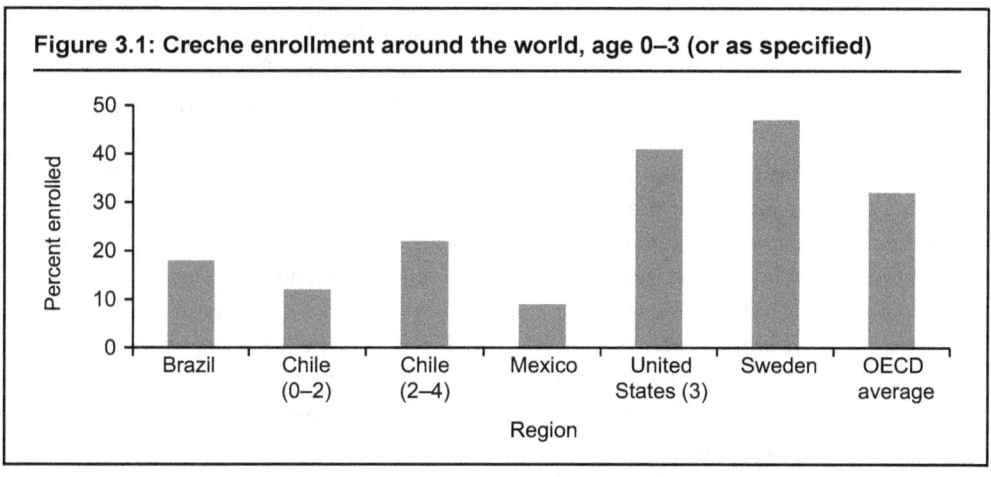

Source: Brazil data from PNAD 2009. U.S. data from Aud et al. (2010). Other data adapted from (Bruns et al. 2010).

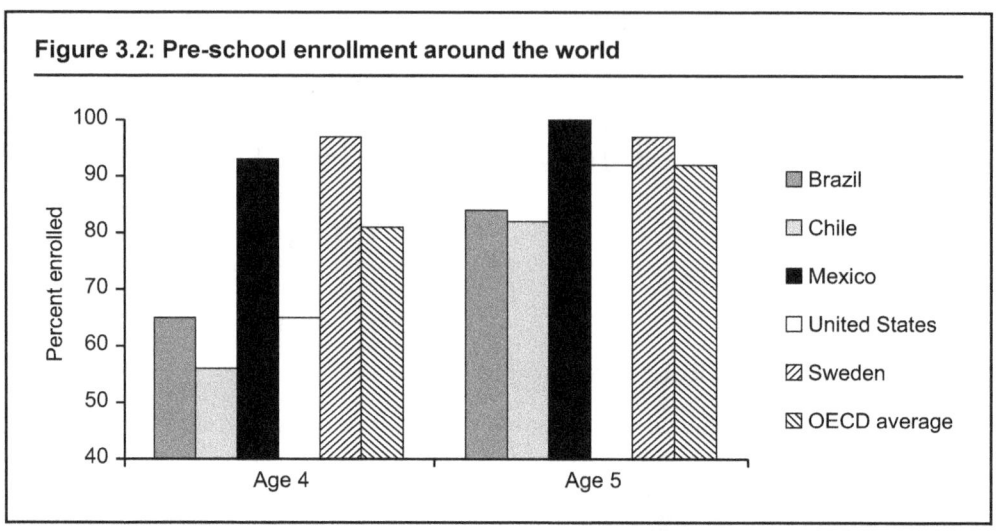

Figure 3.2: Pre-school enrollment around the world

Source: Brazil data from PNAD 2009. Chile data calculated from Mineduc 2010. Data from U.S. Census Bureau, Current Population Survey, October 2009. Other data adapted from Bruns et al. (2010).

effect, although there is evidence that some of the states with the strongest pre-school coverage also have weak creche coverage. A second result in Mexico is that the expansion led to reductions in some quality measures: the proportion of pre-schools with a student-adult ratio exceeding 30 rose significantly in the course of the expansion (Yoshikawa et al. 2007). As Brazil seeks to expand enrollment in coming years, it will need to carefully monitor quality to ensure that access does not leave children in low-quality care.

How Has Access to Early Child Education Evolved in Brazil?

Attendance at creches and pre-schools has increased dramatically in recent years. Only 9 percent of under-four children attended a creche in 1999, but 18 percent attended a creche in 2009—a doubling of the creche enrollment rate over a single decade (figure 3.3).[1] Similarly, while 52 percent of children ages 4–6 attended school in 1999, 81 percent attended school in 2009 (figure 3.4).[2]

This rapid expansion is comparable to expansions in other countries over the same period. While pre-school enrollment expanded by 56 percent in Brazil from 1996 to 2009, pre-school in Colombia expanded by 40 percent, and pre-school in Mexico expanded by 61 percent.

It is immediately clear that pre-school attendance is far more common than is creche attendance. However, while the pre-school enrollment rate was more than six times the enrollment rate in creches in 1996, it was only 4.4 times the creche enrollment rate in 2009. Thus, while pre-school is the more common type of ECE, creches are gaining ground. Although all regions have increased their creche and pre-school enrollment in recent years, there are stark differences across regions. The South and the Southeast had the highest initial creche enrollment rates in 1996 and went on to experience the greatest percentage point increases in enrollment through 2009. The Southeast additionally experienced the largest *percentage* increase in creche enrollment of any region. This has increased the regional gap in creche attendance as the regions that started out with lower enrollment are expanding enrollment more slowly than are the South and the Southeast. In contrast,

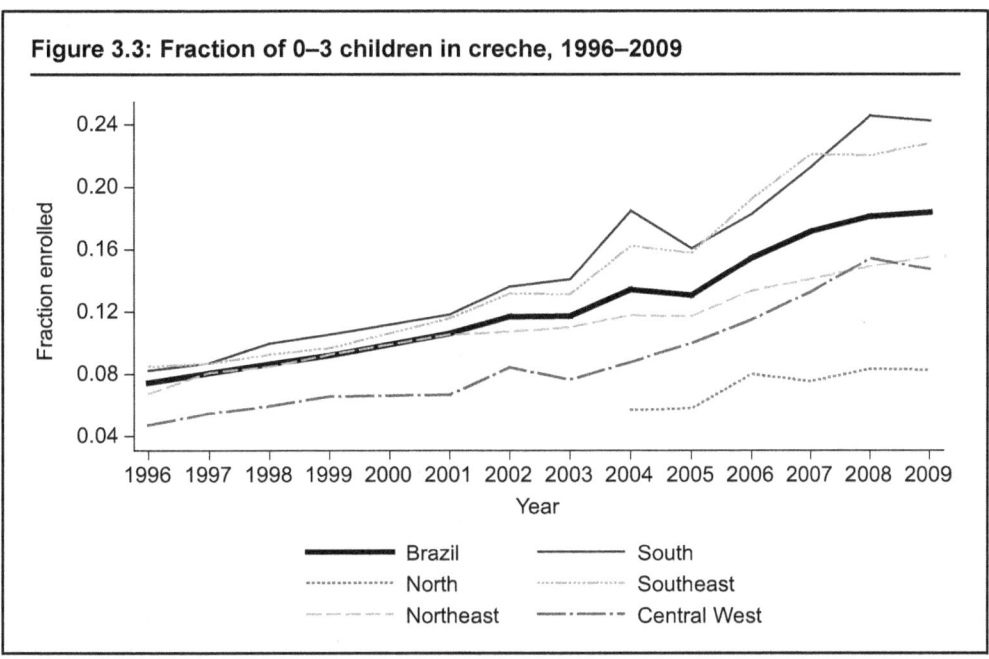

Source: Pesquisa Nacional por Amostra de Domicilios (PNAD), 1996–2009.

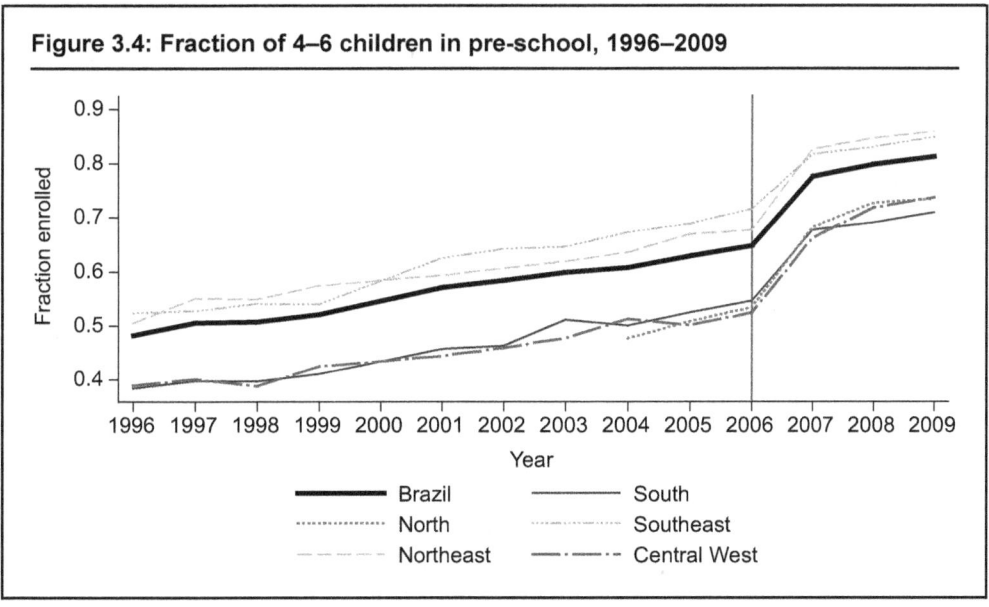

Source: Pesquisa Nacional por Amostra de Domicilios (PNAD), 1996–2009.
Note: Before 2007, this is the pre-school enrollment rate for children aged 4–6. Beginning in 2007, this is the enrollment rate in pre-school and/or the 1st year of primary school for children aged 4–6.

the regional gap in pre-school attendance has decreased slightly since 1996. The Central West and the South—the regions with the lowest pre-school attendance rates in 1996— saw the greatest percentage increase in attendance during 1996–2009. While regional gaps persist, there is convergence.

Regional trends in ECE expansion do not merely track income. The Northeast—one of Brazil's poorest regions—has had higher creche and pre-school enrollment rates than the relatively rich Central West during nearly all of 1996–2009, and has enjoyed some of the highest pre-school enrollment rates of any region. Municipality-specific priorities and levels of demand seem to be important factors driving these investments. Thus, beyond the need for resources, there must be a will to invest as well.

At the state level, there are also stark disparities in access to creches and pre-schools. Figure 3.5 offers a cross-state comparison of access to creches in 2009, and figure 3.6 shows the same for pre-schools. A number of states stand out when compared to others in the same region. For example, Roraima in the North has a creche enrollment rate of 14 percent, which is higher than the rest of the region, and a pre-school enrollment rate of 81 percent, which is close to that of the Federal District. On the other hand, Alagoas, in the Northeast, lags behind the rest of the region in both creche and pre-school enrollment.

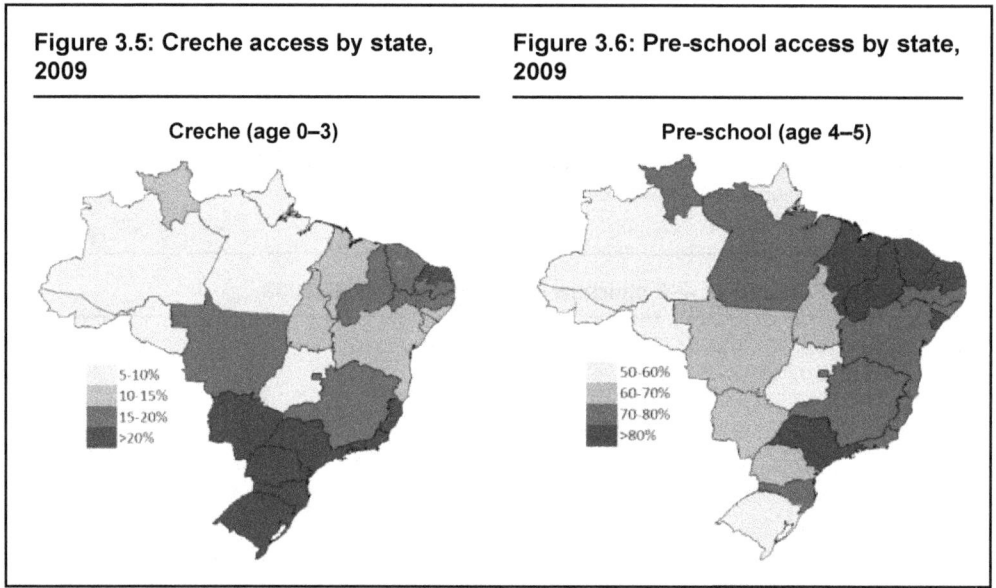

Figure 3.5: Creche access by state, 2009

Figure 3.6: Pre-school access by state, 2009

Source: Data from PNAD (2009).
Note: Creche access is the enrollment rate in schools for children aged 0–3. Pre-school access is the enrollment rate in schools for children aged 4–5.

One of the most important state-level findings is that six states have pre-school enrollment rates of *under 60 percent:* Acre, Amapá, Amazonas, Goiás, Rio Grande do Sul, and Rondônia. That means that, in those states, massive expansions will be necessary in the coming years to achieve universal coverage by 2016.

State-level growth rates of creche and pre-school enrollments between 1996 and 2009 are highly correlated. Generally, states that have boosted creche enrollments have achieved the same with pre-school enrollments, and those that are lagging in one area lag in the other as well. Yet it is also likely that some regions with limited ECE budgets are forced to trade off investment in one level of ECE for investment in another, as Mexico did in its recent, rapid pre-school expansion. In Brazil, the South is an interesting example; while it was the region with the lowest pre-school enrollment rate for several years during 1996–2009, it also enjoyed the highest creche enrollment rate for most of that same period. (Pre-school enrollment is still much higher than creche enrollment.) As both levels of ECE are controlled by the same level of government (the municipality), this suggests that the demand for pre-schools compared to creches varies across regions.

These findings underscore the need to explore how income, urbanization, and female labor force participation have influenced ECE enrollments. These are factors on which regions and states differ markedly, and which likely account for variance in the rate of expansion of ECE.

Gender and ECE

There is little evidence of unequal access to ECE for boys versus girls. In general, differences in attendance by gender appear to be temporary and non-systematic (figure 3.7 and figure 3.8). For both creches and pre-schools, none of Brazil's regions has consistently had higher attendance by boys than by girls, or vice versa, during the last decade. This is consistent with broader education attendance patterns in Brazil, which show little evidence of gender disparities.

Poor children are being left behind

While children of all income quintiles attend creches and pre-schools, access is most highly-concentrated among the wealthiest (figure 3.9). This may be true for several reasons. First, in areas with a high concentration of high-income families, the tax base from which public education is funded will be relatively larger. This is especially true in Brazil. Municipalities legally must spend at least 25 percent of their revenue on education. Higher revenue automatically translates into higher education spending. Even though the 1998 FUNDEF—and the subsequent 2007 FUNDEB—reform partially equalized education spending, it did so *within* states, which meant that municipalities in wealthier states still enjoyed more education resources than did those in poorer states. The federal

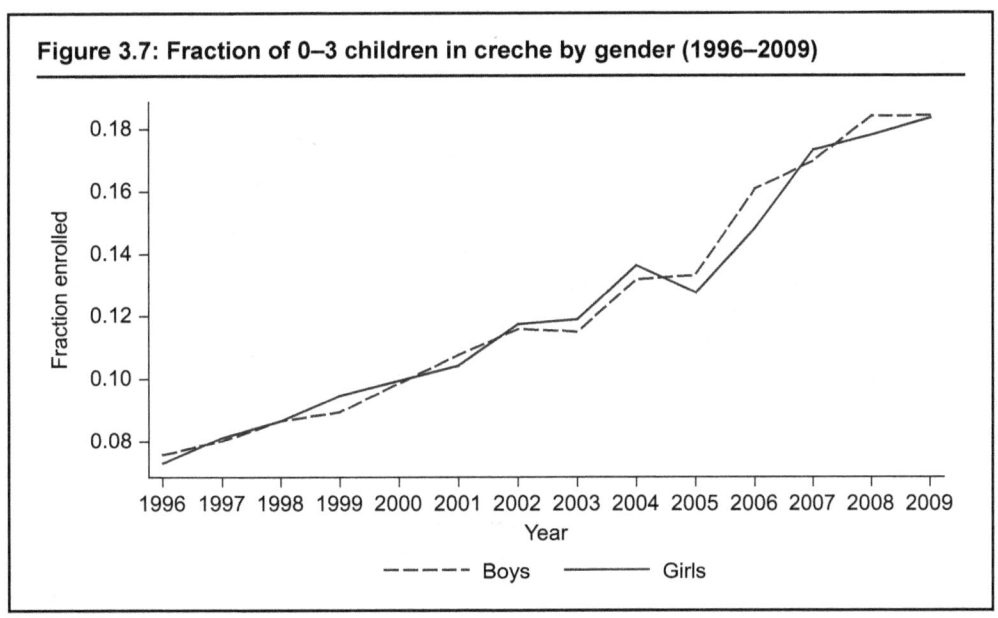

Figure 3.7: Fraction of 0–3 children in creche by gender (1996–2009)

Source: Pesquisa Nacional por Amostra de Domicilios (PNAD), 1996–2009.

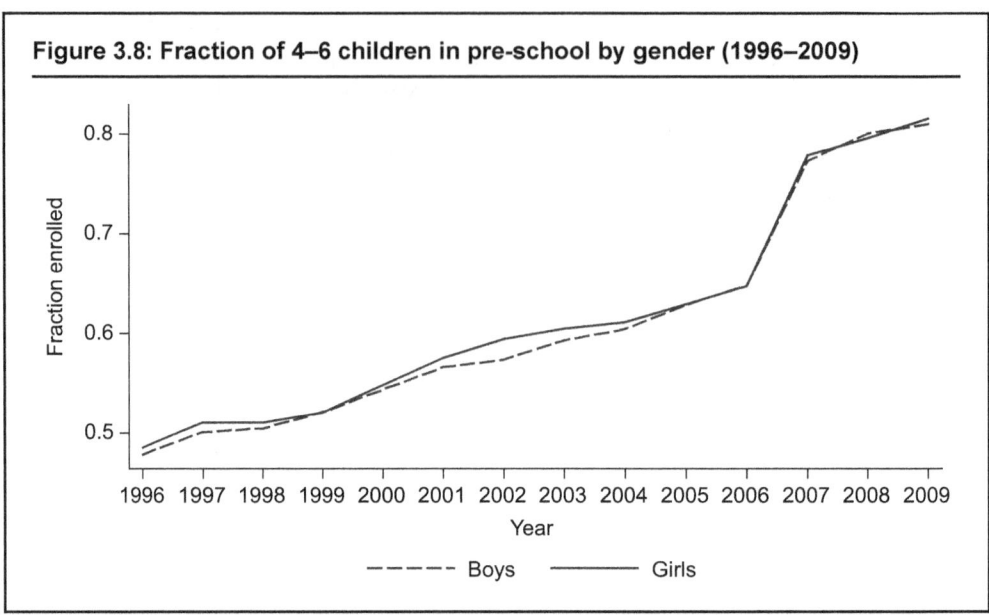

Figure 3.8: Fraction of 4–6 children in pre-school by gender (1996–2009)

Source: Pesquisa Nacional por Amostra de Domicilios (PNAD), 1996–2009.
Note: Before 2007, 6 year olds are pre-school-aged. Beginning in 2007, 6 year olds are in first grade.

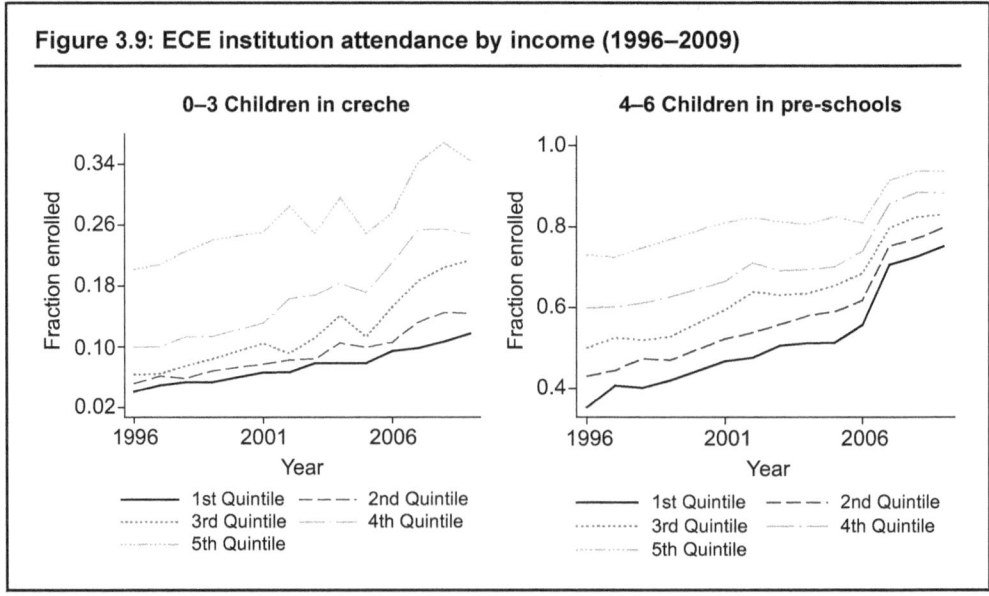

Figure 3.9: ECE institution attendance by income (1996–2009)

Source: Pesquisa Nacional por Amostra de Domicilios (PNAD), 1996–2009.
Note: Before 2007, the pre-school attendance rate is the fraction of 4–6 year olds in pre-school. Beginning in 2007, the pre-school attendance rate is the fraction of 4–6 year olds in institutions intended for 4–6 year olds.

government topped off the education funds in states that did not meet a per-student minimum, but this only benefitted some states, and did not close the education financing gap between states. Second, families' ability to pay rises with family income. High income families can afford private early child education where public education is absent or of low quality. Third, because parental income and parental education are positively correlated, children from higher-income families are also more likely to have parents who place a high intrinsic value on education. Such parents may be more likely to enroll their children in early child education. Finally, children from higher-income families are less likely to need to work to help support their families. While child labor among children ages 0–5 is uncommon in Brazil, it does occur, and could prevent enrollment.

Figure 3.9 reveals not only the strength of the relationship between family income and ECE institution attendance, but also how the situation varies across creches and pre-schools, and how it has changed over time. The income gap in age 4–6 attendance at school appears to be narrowing while the income gap in age 0–3 attendance is expanding. This is likely due to the fact that, beginning in 2007, six-year-olds were gradually brought into primary school, which is a compulsory level of education. When all children—rich and poor—must be provided a space in a public school, family income naturally has less of an impact on school attendance. Given a 2009 constitutional amendment to initiate mandatory schooling at age four, the income gap in pre-school attendance is likely to fall even further in the coming years. The case of primary and lower-secondary education—which have been mandatory for decades—suggests such an outcome. As of 2009, 99 percent of the wealthiest 6–14 year olds attended school, but the poorest children were not far behind, with an attendance rate of 96 percent.

Wealthier families are not only more likely to enroll their children in ECE; they are also much more likely to use the private system (figure 3.10 and figure 3.11). At the bottom quintile of per capita household income, 85 percent of parents use public creches and 92 percent use public pre-schools. In contrast, at the top quintile, 81 percent use private creches and 74 percent use private pre-schools. Private ECE not only costs money, but—as shown later—it tends to be of higher quality on several dimensions. If public ECE is not available, or if it is of low quality, a poor family may have no other option than to keep a child at home.

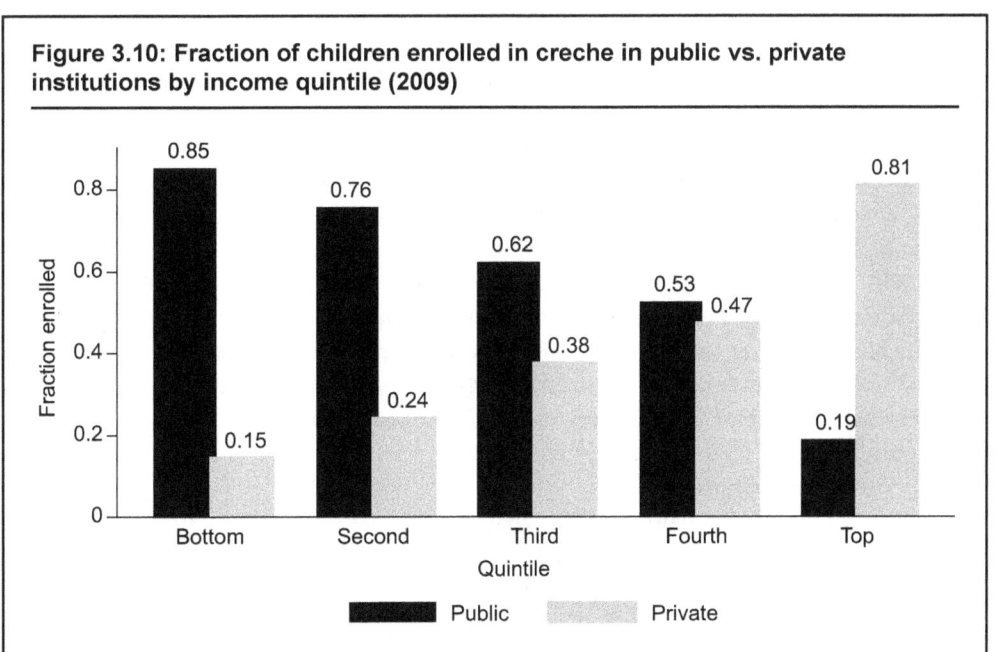

Figure 3.10: Fraction of children enrolled in creche in public vs. private institutions by income quintile (2009)

Source: Pesquisa Nacional por Amostra de Domicilios (PNAD), 1996–2009.

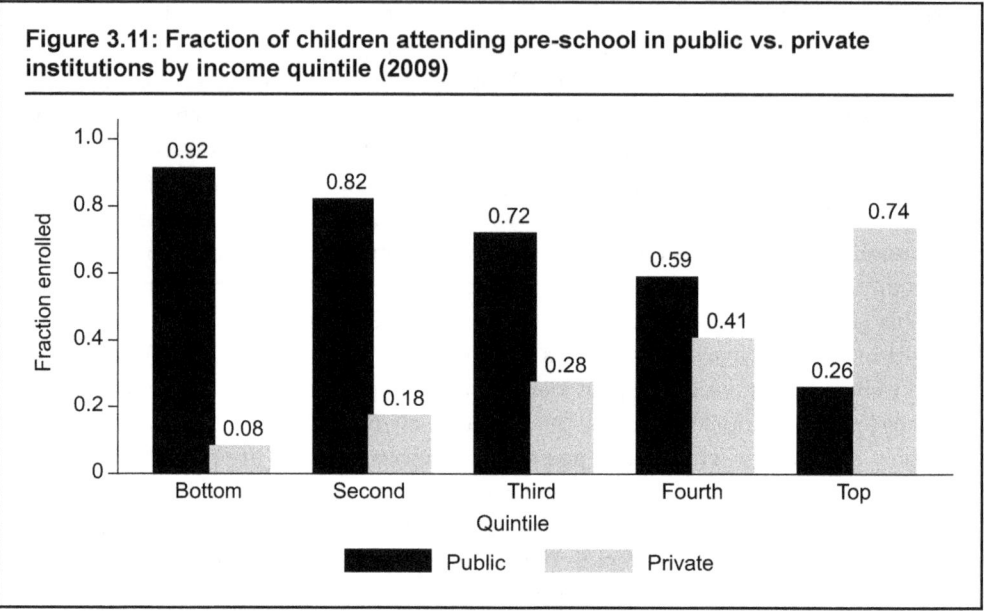

Figure 3.11: Fraction of children attending pre-school in public vs. private institutions by income quintile (2009)

Source: Pesquisa Nacional por Amostra de Domicilios (PNAD), 1996–2009.

Rural children are being left behind

Creche and pre-school enrollment are also less common in rural areas. Urban households have higher incomes (more than double as of 2009), which likely explains part of the gap. As described above, this has an effect on the education budget in the municipality. It also has an effect on parents' ability to self-finance early child education. Rural areas may also have longer or more complicated commutes to centers or schools, which can be difficult for young children. Gaps in access between urban and rural areas provide unequal opportunities to children based on their geographic location. Vega and Barros (2011) demonstrate that living in a rural area is one of the main sources of exclusion in accessing housing services and amenities like electricity, water, and sanitation. They also show that socioeconomic status is a huge source of exclusion in accessing pre-school and other basic education, housing, and health services, and in progressing successfully through school. Given that rural areas are generally poor, a large share of rural children—for a multitude of reasons—lacks opportunities to succeed. Policies that can creatively expand early child education in rural areas which cannot be served by center-based care or other common modalities can help to overcome these unequal opportunities.

The rural-urban pre-school enrollment gap is narrowing (figure 3.12). However, as figure 3.13 demonstrates, rural children ages 4–6 in the highest two income quintiles are about as likely to attend school as are urban children the same age in the lowest two income quintiles. That is, the *wealthiest* rural children attend creche at about the same rate as the *poorest* urban children.

Figure 3.13 suggests that the rural-urban gap in pre-school attendance cannot be attributed to the relative poverty of rural areas alone. It may also be the case that children in rural areas have access to more reliable forms of informal child care—such as neighborhood cooperatives, relatives, and care by trusted friends—than do children in urban areas. Finally, female participation in the labor force is slightly less common in rural

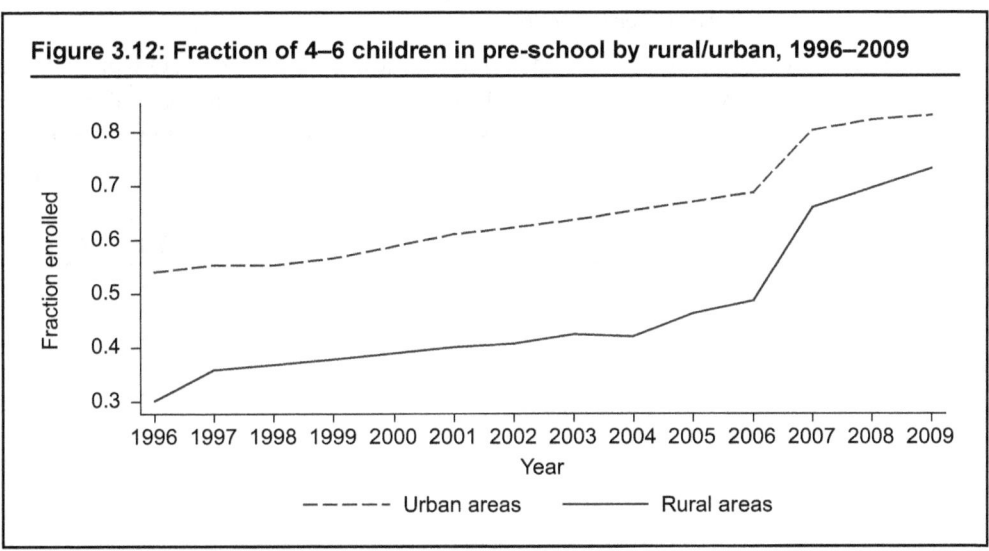

Figure 3.12: Fraction of 4–6 children in pre-school by rural/urban, 1996–2009

Source: Pesquisa Nacional por Amostra de Domicilios (PNAD), 1996–2009.
Note: Before 2007, 6 year olds are pre-school-aged. Beginning in 2007, 6 year olds are in first grade.

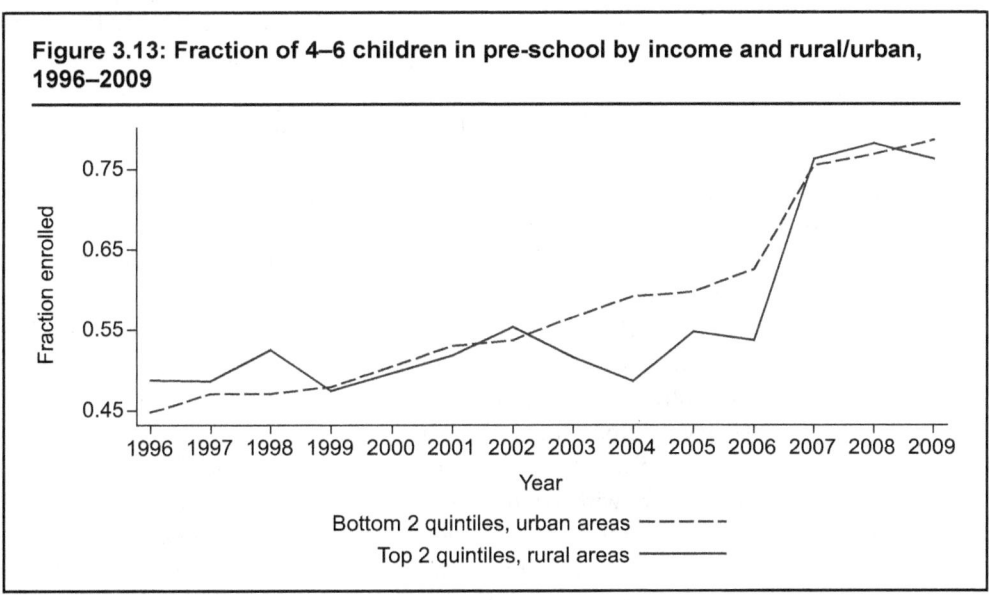

Figure 3.13: Fraction of 4–6 children in pre-school by income and rural/urban, 1996–2009

Source: Pesquisa Nacional por Amostra de Domicilios (PNAD), 1996–2009
Note: Before 2007, 6 year olds are pre-school-aged. Beginning in 2007, 6 year olds are in first grade.

areas than in urban areas of Brazil. In 2009, 40 percent of mothers of 0–3 children in rural areas worked, whereas 43 percent of mothers of 0–3 children worked in urban areas (including both formal and informal work). Similarly, in 2009, 48 percent of mothers of 4–6 children in rural areas worked, but 50 percent of mothers of 4–6 children in urban areas did. Although these differences are small, the low levels of creche participation in rural areas mean that even small increases in female labor force participation that translate into higher creche enrollments could result in significant percentage expansions.

Female labor force participation (FLFP) and early child education

At the same time that ECE enrollment has been expanding, more and more women have been joining the labor force. Labor force participation in Brazil tops 60 percent, which is higher than the Latin American average, and is comparable to OECD countries (table 3.1).

Table 3.1: Labor force participation across countries

Country	1996	2008	Growth: 1996–2008
Brazil	52%	60%	16%
Colombia	33%	41%	23%
Chile	35%	44%	25%
Mexico	38%	43%	16%
Latin America & Caribbean	44%	52%	16%
United States	59%	59%	0%
Sweden	60%	61%	2%

Source: World Development Indicators, World Bank.

The labor force participation (LFP) for mothers of young children in particular has expanded dramatically, faster than the average for Brazil or the region. LFP among mothers of creche-age children has risen from 33 percent in 1998 to 42 percent in 2007, a 27 percent increase. LFP among mothers of pre-school age children has risen from 41 percent to 48 percent, a 17 percent increase (just above the Brazil and regional average of 16 percent).

Publicly-provided child care has been shown internationally to increase female labor supply, and evidence from Brazil supports this finding. A recent study in Rio de Janeiro (described in box 2.2) compares mothers of children who were provided spaces in public creches to mothers of children who were not. A lottery determined entry, so mothers from both groups of children are comparable. Among mothers not working prior to the study, the employment rate eight months later of mothers receiving public care was double that of mothers not receiving care: 17 percent versus 9 percent (Barros et al. 2011b). Thus, a policy of expanding creches provides some of the resources to pay for itself by significantly expanding the number of women in the labor force.

Fewer than half of mothers with young children (0–3) in Brazil work, although the numbers are expanding. Higher rates of FLFP among mothers of pre-school-aged children than among mothers of creche-aged children indicate greater preference for at-home care of very young children, as well as higher costs of safely transporting very young children and labor market difficulties that stem from taking time off for childbirth and early infancy. Maternity leave in Brazil is four months, but it is currently being raised to six months. This expansion may allow new mothers to better retain an existing job, which would then increase the need for creche spaces in the years following maternity leave.

Even non-working mothers have become significantly more likely to send their children to creches over the last decade. The fact that creche enrollments are expanding among non-working mothers suggests that age 0–3 ECE is seen to offer benefits beyond maternal labor force participation. However, the gap in creche attendance rates between children with working and with non-working mothers has expanded from eight to fifteen percentage points between 1996 and 2009, as shown in figure 3.14.[3] Creche enrollment is thus increasingly associated with a mother's working status. And yet, less than one-third of children with working mothers are in a creche. Where are those children? Presumably, they are in the care of fathers, older relatives at home, or neighbors. For example, many households with a grandparent living at home do not send their children to creche (INEP 2009).

Working and non-working mothers have made similar gains in enrolling children in pre-school over the last decade. The enrollment gap between the children of working and non-working mothers has actually narrowed slightly (figure 3.15). This decrease may be in part attributable to the gradual incorporation of six-year-olds into primary

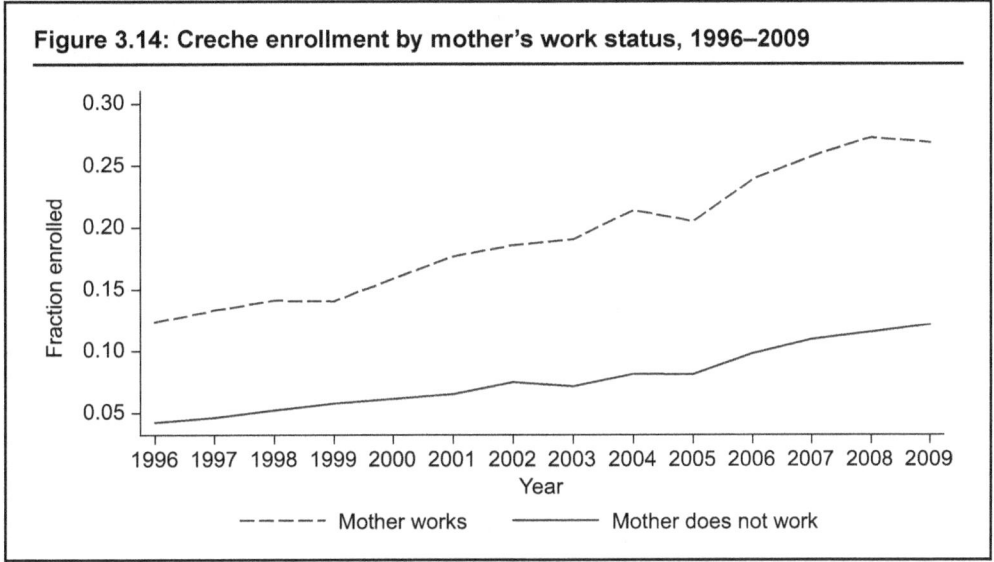

Source: Pesquisa Nacional por Amostra de Domicilios (PNAD), 1996–2009.

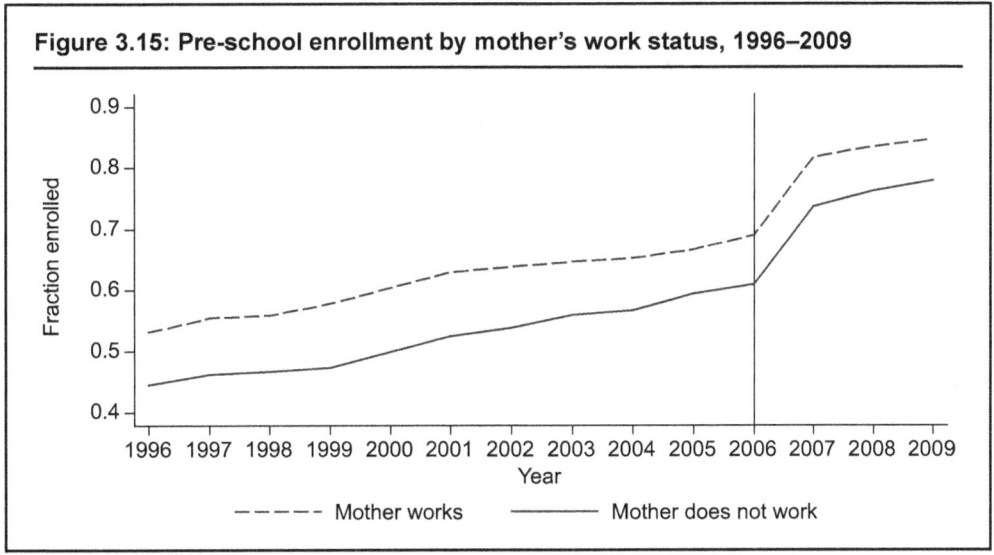

Source: Pesquisa Nacional por Amostra de Domicilios (PNAD), 1996–2009.
Note: Before 2007, 6 year olds are pre-school-aged. Beginning in 2007, 6 year olds are in first grade.

education starting in 2007, for which attendance—being required—is less dependent on mothers' employment status. However, the gap was already narrowing in the decade between 1996 and 2006, perhaps because schooling for six-year-olds (and even for 4–5 year-olds) became more of a norm.

Reaching the Poorest: How Many to Plan For

Given that pre-school education is now compulsory, and municipalities must come into compliance by 2016, the Ministry of Education's goal is universal enrollment by 2016 (Weber 2011). As highlighted earlier, Brazil has a significant gap to close in order to achieve that goal. Six states have less than 60 percent of children enrolled in pre-schools, and an additional 13 states have less than 80 percent enrolled. The total number of children not yet enrolled is striking (table 3.2). Yet that number is expected to fall significantly over the next fifteen years—in part due to Brazil's fertility decline over the past 25 years. Enrollments in elementary school (Ensino Fundamental) are also expected to drop 23 percent over the same period, freeing up resources to achieve larger-scale ECE enrollments.

Table 3.2: Total number of children not enrolled in ECE, by region

Region	Creche-aged children (0–3) not enrolled		Pre-school-aged children (4–5) not enrolled	
	2009	2025	2009	2025
North	1,190,368	964,198	247,577	188,159
Northeast	3,101,091	2,511,884	360,118	273,690
South	3,410,352	2,762,385	316,093	240,231
Southeast	1,141,513	924,626	482,143	366,429
Central West	749,702	607,259	164,581	125,082
Brazil	9,593,026	7,770,351	1,570,512	1,193,589

Sources: PNAD (2009) survey data, IBGE (2009) population data, and IBGE (2007) population-by-age estimates.

In order to reach this magnitude of children, Brazil will need to incorporate an array of delivery mechanisms. Three-quarters of the 1.6 million 4–5 year olds not in pre-school and much of the creche access gap lie in urban areas (see table 3.3) where construction of new centers or adaptation of buildings into centers may be the most efficient solution.

Yet coverage rates are much lower in rural areas. In some rural areas, population densities are such that filling an average-sized pre-school or creche may require too much travel for very young children to justify center-based education. Table 3.5 shows the average size of pre-schools, in terms of the number of students, by region. In São Paulo state, 0.4 km² of territory in São Paulo municipality would be sufficient to fill an average-sized São Paulo pre-school with 4–5 year olds.[4] However, in more rural Barra do Turvo municipality, also in São Paulo state, over 320 km² would be required to fill an average-sized pre-school. Similarly, in Pernambuco state, 0.15 km² in Recife municipality would be sufficient to fill an average-sized Pernambuco pre-school with 4–5 year olds. However, in more rural Parnamirim municipality, the same pre-school would have to serve over 110 km² of territory. Due to economies of scale, it is inevitably more expensive to expand early child education in more rural municipalities. In those areas, the challenge is to either create cost-effective center-based care on a smaller-than-typical scale, or to use home visits and other delivery modalities that might be more suited to rural areas.

Table 3.3: Number of 4–5 year olds not enrolled in pre-school in 2009, by rural/urban and region

Region	Children not enrolled, urban areas	Children not enrolled, rural areas	Fraction of children not enrolled that are in urban areas (%)
North	157,152	90,425	63
Northeast	215,662	144,456	60
South	247,635	68,458	78
Southeast	393,718	88,425	82
Central West	135,348	29,233	82
Brazil	1,149,515	420,997	73

Sources: PNAD (2009) survey data, IBGE (2009) population data, and IBGE (2007) population-by-age estimates.

The policy goal for creche enrollments is less clear. According to the 1988 constitution, creche care is a right.[5] Yet not all families want to enroll their young children in center-based care, especially in the earliest years. Further, there is no evidence that universal creche care would be beneficial. Almost all the international evidence is for pre-school, and the evidence that does exist for earlier ages has clearer positive results for highly vulnerable households. What is the ideal enrollment rate?

The public provision target rate for children ages 0–3 for European Union countries, set out in the 2002 Barcelona EU meeting, is 33 percent. The rationale for the target, however, is focused on providing working opportunities for women rather than on child development (European Council Conclusions 2002). A more recent UNICEF report, seeking to establish benchmarks for early childhood services in OECD countries, proposes a target of 25 percent of children ages 0–3, reducing the EU target so that countries can focus on ensuring that all care is licensed and regulated (Bennett 2008). In Brazil, the National Plan for Education, passed into law in 2001, set a goal of 30 percent creche enrollment by 2005 and 50 percent enrollment by 2010. The new National Plan for Education extends the deadline for that 50 percent enrollment target to 2020. The collaborative National Plan for Early Childhood, coordinated by the National Network for Early Childhood[6] and developed in concert with a broad range of government and non-government institutions, calls for 40 percent enrollment of children ages 0–3 by 2016, and 70 percent enrollment by 2022. These are clearly more ambitious than the EU and OECD targets.

To plan their growth and investment strategies, municipalities need to know the unmet demand for creches. One strategy to estimate demand, proposed by researchers at IPEA, examines the take-up rate of creche care among the wealthiest segment of the population, as this population faces a weak budgetary constraint to ECE enrollment (Barros et al. 2010). Creche use in Brazil is more than three times as high for the richest fifth of the population as for the poorest fifth (34 percent versus 11 percent, shown in figure 3.9). In the highly urban municipality of Rio de Janeiro, about 52 percent of the wealthiest fifth of the population and 20 percent of the poorest fifth are enrolled. Attendance by the wealthiest 5 percent of the population is similar to that of the wealthiest 20 percent. In other words, the wealthiest households in Rio de Janeiro—whether defined narrowly or broadly—send their children to creches about half the time (figure 3.16).

Of course, using the wealthiest families to calculate the creche demand of the poorest has potential problems. On the one hand, poorer families may have less access to substitute services like nannies; on the other hand, they may have more underemployed

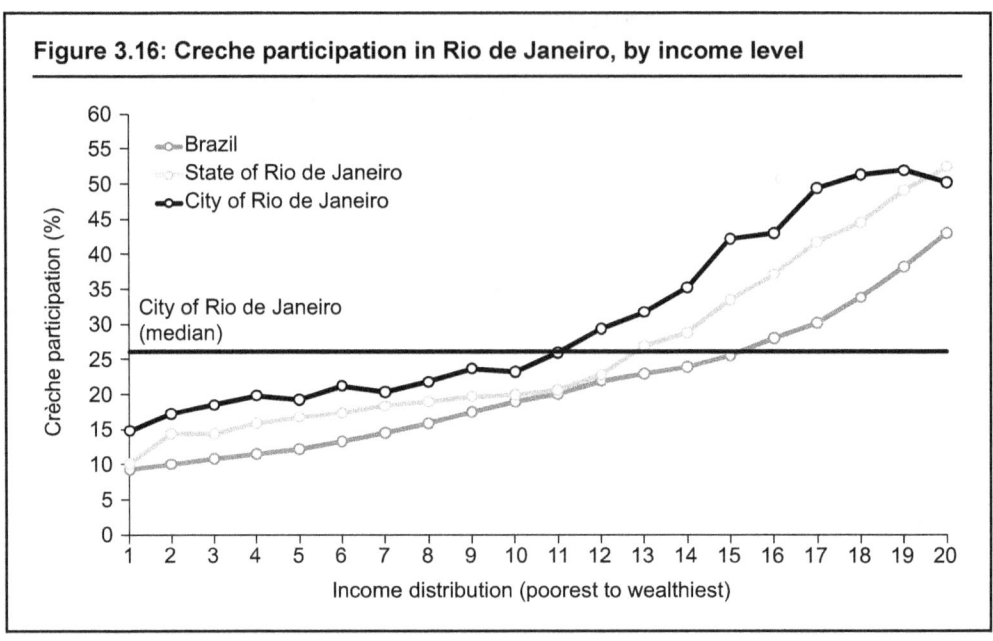

Figure 3.16: Creche participation in Rio de Janeiro, by income level

Source: Pesquisa Nacional por Amostra de Domicilios (PNAD), 2006–08.

relatives to provide child care service. Also, female participation in the workforce is higher among the wealthiest (although this may in part be driven by access to childcare). Nonetheless, one can learn much about potential unmet demand for creche services among poorer families by assuming that their overall demand is similar to the expressed demand for these services by wealthier families.

Creche enrollment rates of children ages 0–3 in the richest fifth of households vary across Brazil's regions, from 25 percent in the Central West to 43 percent in the South, as shown in table 3.4. Using the assumption that these numbers represent the share of parents in each of these regions desiring their age 0–3 children to be enrolled in center-based programs would imply demand for creche care of approximately 4 million children. At this point, about 2.2 million children ages 0–3 are enrolled in creche, so satisfying remaining demand would require a near doubling of spaces. However, unmet need (as calculated using this method) varies across regions. In the Southeast, 34 percent of demand is currently unmet, whereas this is true for 66 percent of demand in the North.[7]

Table 3.4: Estimated demand for creche, by region

Region	Enrollment rate of children 0–3, richest 20% of households	Total children 0–3	Total estimated demand for creche spaces	Children currently enrolled	Unmet demand
North	24%	1,297,686	312,772	107,318	205,454
Northeast	34%	3,670,508	1,235,395	569,417	665,978
Southeast	35%	4,417,646	1,534,584	1,007,294	527,290
South	43%	1,506,833	643,875	365,320	278,555
Central West	25%	879,147	224,171	129,445	94,726

Source: Censo Escolar (2009) and IBGE Censo (2000).

These differences have implications for any national policy that aims to expand creche spaces where unmet demand is greatest. If universal access to pre-school is the goal, Brazil cannot make similarly-sized investments in all regions. Investments need to target areas with the greatest unmet need.

Building New Centers

Municipalities are continually constructing new early child education centers, causing a rapid rise in creche and pre-school enrollments throughout the country: from just over half a million public creche enrollments in 2001 to almost five million in 2009. The total number of public creches has nearly doubled, from 13,382 to 24,731 over the same period (figure 3.17). The number of pre-schools also grew over that time period, but comparability is complicated by the change in the eligible age for pre-school, from 4–6 previously to 4–5 in 2007. Policy makers across Brazil face the important questions of how many centers to build and where to build them.

In Brazil, the average pre-school has 45 students, although the regional average varies from 71 in the Southeast to 32 in the Northeast (table 3.5). If additional pre-schools of

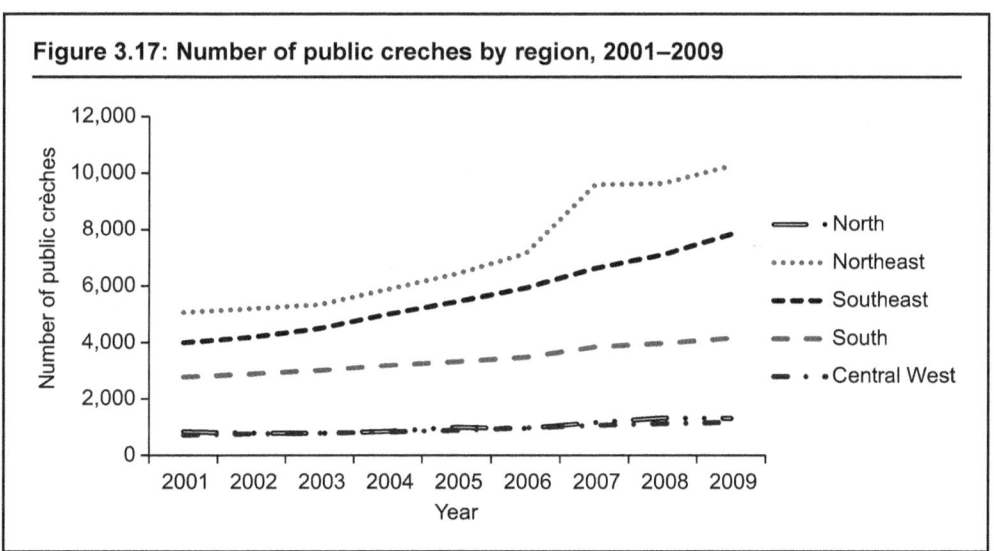

Source: PNAD (2009) survey data.

Table 3.5: Average enrollment size of pre-schools in 2009, by region

Region	Average size of pre-schools (enrollment)	Additional pre-schools required to reach universal enrollment of 4–5 year olds
North	44	5,400
Northeast	32	11,535
South	40	8,098
Southeast	71	6,887
Central West	63	2,563
Brazil	45	34,812

Sources: PNAD (2009) survey data, Census of Schools (2009) school-level data, IBGE (2009) population data, and IBGE (2007) population-by-age estimates.

these average sizes were built in each region to accommodate all un-enrolled 4–5 year-olds, almost 35,000 new pre-schools would be needed.

This again points to the need to not only construct additional centers, but also to explore alternative mechanisms for reaching some of Brazil's children.

Targeting

At the pre-school level, the goal is universal enrollment by 2016. At the creche level, where universal access (but not necessarily enrollment) is the goal, municipalities must prioritize given that enrollment was only 18 percent nationwide in 2009. Indeed, better targeting will alleviate some of the immediate demand for expansion. For example, in the municipality of Rio de Janeiro, the need to expand in order to satisfy demand for spaces among just the poorest half of the population is 90 percent under current targeting, but that includes many creche spaces going to wealthy children whose families could afford to self-finance creche care. Meanwhile, if those public spaces were given to the poorest, then Rio would only need to expand by 69 percent in order to satisfy demands for the poor—still a tall order, but more plausible.

The same problem holds across Brazil. In public creches, 13 percent of scarce spots are taken by children from the richest families (figure 3.10). If those same spaces were allocated to the poorest 20 percent, then overall enrollment in creche amongst the poorest would increase by half. This misallocation of scarce spaces has not improved: it has hovered around 20 percent for almost a decade, from 2002. Furthermore, the evidence presented in Chapter One demonstrated that the returns to early child education are particularly high for the poorest and most vulnerable households; these households have the fewest resources to fund child development-promoting alternatives to public creches.

Given the importance of targeting, how should a municipality assign its scarce spaces? The method most municipalities currently use to allocate spaces is completely decentralized, as each creche director is responsible for assigning spaces. A second method, less used in Brazil, but more effective from a resource allocation standpoint, is to have a centralized, means-tested selection process at the municipal level. A third method, which the Municipality of Rio de Janeiro adopted for cohorts entering creches from 2008 through 2010, is to use a lottery to allot scarce spaces among equally eligible families. These methods are discussed below.

Decentralized selection. Many municipalities permit creche directors to make their own decisions, often based on provided (but not enforced) guidelines. This was the experience in Rio de Janeiro prior to 2007. As a result, creche directors used their discretion and the process was not very systematic. An investigation revealed wide variation in the criteria actually employed to admit children into creches, despite the general guidelines. The advantage of this method is that it permits directors to identify those children who may slip through the cracks of a formal selection process. The disadvantage is that directors may fail to be objective when it is efficient to do so, or they may even be biased against children with special needs or developmental delays that require more involved or expensive care.

Means-tested selection. A second method is to use a process to identify the children in greatest need, and to select them. One natural approach would be to employ the social protection register (*cadastro único*). To improve targeting, the government of Rio de Janeiro recently adopted a means-tested selection process. Specifically, the government decided that children in Cartão Carioca (a Rio de Janeiro-specific supplement to Bolsa Familia) would be given highest priority, with levels of vulnerability determining access in the case of excess demand within that group. In the first year of implementation, all of the neediest children—those in Cartão Carioca—whose parents solicited creche spots received them. The advantage of this method is that it is much more likely to identify the most vulnerable children than is decentralized selection. However, some highly vulnerable children who do not fit the particular criteria may be excluded. This problem might be ameliorated by allowing directors a certain share of vacancies over which they do have discretion.

Lottery-based selection. Some creches in Brazil use a lottery to assign scarce spaces. In Bahia, one government creche uses a simple lottery with a certain number of spaces reserved for public servants (Governo da Bahia 2011). The municipality of Rio de Janeiro implemented a lottery for the entering creche classes of 2008–2010, allowing any child an opportunity to participate in a creche, but providing higher odds for children from the most vulnerable backgrounds. (In 2011 the lottery was replaced with a simple means-tested formula, giving priority to participants of Cartão Carioca, the Rio de Janeiro supplement to Bolsa Familia.) Public creches were built in vulnerable areas of Rio de Janeiro, so they already targeted the most vulnerable children given that households in wealthier areas were unlikely to want to travel far or into lower-income parts of the city for care.[8]

One of the advantages of the lottery system is that it provides every interested child with the possibility of a space in a creche. Because no testing of children's socioeconomic status is perfect, this means that even children who are judged less vulnerable by standard indicators but who perhaps have some particular, less visible need, may earn a place. In addition, a lottery leads to more diversity in socioeconomic background across children in the creches. On the other hand, this method means that a proportion of creche spaces go to children that are not in the most vulnerable groups.

What kind of centers?

As municipalities seek to construct new centers, a key question is what kind of centers to build? Creches and pre-schools can be expansions of existing primary schools, self-contained early child education centers, and—in some cases—may have no formal school building at all (e.g., they are located in a church or in someone's home). Over the past five years, the vast majority of growth has occurred through adding creches and pre-schools to existing primary schools, as shown in table 3.6.

Table 3.6: ECE institutions, by type of institution (2005, 2009)

Creches	2005	2009	Growth (%)
In school building with only early child education	19,447	22,887	18
In school building with other education levels	8,732	16,338	87
Not in a formal school building	4,117	3,805	−8
Total	32,296	43,030	33
Pre-schools			
In school building with only early child education	24,099	23,513	−2
In school building with other education levels	71,670	74,630	4
Not in a formal school building	9,847	8,420	−14
Total	105,616	106,563	1

Sources: PNAD (2009) survey data, Census of Schools (2009) school-level data, IBGE (2009) population data, and IBGE (2007) population-by-age estimates.

Adding ECE to existing schools is more cost-effective than constructing entirely new buildings, most strikingly with regards to the challenges of acquiring new land versus expanding construction on land already managed by the municipal government. However, evidence supports the value of dedicated early child development centers, called EDIs (espaços de desenvolvimento infantil). A recent study of ECE center quality in six Brazilian capitals that judges quality using observational tools covering activities, infrastructure, interactions, etc., showed that creches and pre-schools had significantly higher quality when housed in their own building than when joined with an elementary school (Fundação Carlos Chagas 2010).[9] Interestingly, the quality differential was three times larger for pre-schools than for creches. The rationale behind this quality improvement is that early child education requires different skills and a different approach than teaching children at higher grade levels; separate ECE institutions have a greater opportunity to organize around a culture of early child education, rather adopting a prevailing elementary school pedagogical culture. Thus, municipalities will have to weigh quality against pragmatism as they seek to expand creches and pre-schools to meet the needs of their citizens.

Placement

Given existing demand, policy makers are left with the question of where to build the creches. A simple combination of the PNAD household survey and the IBGE demographic census allows for neighborhood-by-neighborhood calculations of the ideal location for future early child education centers, following the steps in table 3.7. The calcu-

Table 3.7: Method for identifying locations for new ECE centers

A. Calculate number of children 0–3 by neighborhood [Population Census]
B. Apply demand-rate using take-up rate among the wealthy (50%, in the case of Rio de Janeiro) [PNAD]
C. Apply poverty rate by neighborhood [Population Census]
D. Contrast with existing creche availability by neighborhood [Municipal records]
E. Calculate excess demand among poor by neighborhood

Source: Barros et al. (2010).

lation entails combining estimates on (a) the population of children ages 0 to 3, (b) the percentage of those children with interest in attending creche (extrapolated from the observed enrollment rate of the richest households), and (c) the percentage of the children who—by their level of income—would have claim to free public care. This analysis, carried out for Rio de Janeiro by local researchers, resulted in identification of key neighborhoods in the West Zone of the city (e.g., Campo Grande, Santa Cruz) and in a few other key areas (e.g., Cidade de Deus, Complexo do Alemão). Such analyses can help municipalities target and deliver creche care effectively. Nonetheless, such analyses may be largely limited to metropolitan areas. PNAD data in particular only allow performance of this analysis for whole states or metropolitan areas, and comparable datasets are generally not available for small and rural areas.

Alternative Ways to Deliver Early Child Education

Some states and municipalities are exploring alternative delivery mechanisms, especially for the youngest children. These mechanisms are alternatives to standard, center-based care, and can be used to reach children that cannot be effectively or efficiently reached by standard modalities. The low population density in rural areas, for example, makes alternative methods especially appealing there. Two examples of alternatives are the Primeira Infância Melhor (Better Early Childhood, or PIM) program in the State of Rio Grande do Sul—which focuses on children from birth—and the Asas da Florestania Infantil (Children's Wings of Florestania[10]) or Asinhas program in the state of Acre— which focuses on children of pre-school age.

Primeira Infância Melhor

The most developed example of combined home-based and center-based care for children in Brazil is *Primeira Infância Melhor*, a program based in the Health Secretariat in the state of Rio Grande do Sul. This program, largely modeled on Cuba's Educa a Su Hijo (Educate Your Child) program, provides two modalities of care: (1) individual care for pregnant women and for children from birth to two years, eleven months of age, and (2) group care for pregnant women and for children ages 3–6. For the individual care, an agent visits the home (once a week for children, twice a month for pregnant women) and conducts cognitive stimulation activities as well as child health and development monitoring. For group care, participants meet in a community center, church hall, or other space, and take part in games and activities to stimulate children or prepare expectant mothers for parenthood. Topics include nursing and childbirth, among others (Schneider et al. 2009; Schneider and Ramires 2007).

An evaluation comparing children before and after entry into the program showed significant cognitive, social, and motor development. Likewise, a comparison between children in the same communities who did and did not participate in the program showed strong gains in all of these dimensions (Primeira Infância Melhor 2011).

Asas da Florestania Infantil

The State Education Secretariat in Acre has partnered with several municipalities to offer home-based early child stimulation. One of the major challenges that municipalities in the North face is that children live far from schools, which is problematic for all children, but especially for the youngest. The State of Acre created the Asinhas program in 2009 to reach those in remote areas. This program is directed at children ages 4–5 living in the most inaccessible rural areas, most of them in the heart of the forest.

The program uses a home-based visit strategy to support children's social, psychomotor, and cognitive development. Education agents trained by the State Secretariat of Education make visits twice a week to the homes of children in rural areas. Usually they select one house in a community that will accommodate all of the participating children in the neighborhood. These communities are very isolated, very small and have, on average, five families and around five to seven children ages 4–5. In 2010, 181 education agents reached 1,700 children ages 4–5 and 1,397 families in 15 municipalities in the state (Tribuna 2010). The program is divided into six modules with specific booklets for children, and manuals with guidelines for agents to follow in their interactions with the children and families. Education agents, who are secondary school students or newly graduated teachers, visit the children twice a week in the beginning of the program (module one), and three times a week in the subsequent modules. The municipalities pay their agents and supervisors, and the Education Secretariat provides training, didactic materials, and technical assistance. This program has not been carefully evaluated, and a rigorous evaluation of this model of support would be very welcome.

Provision and Financing of Early Child Education

Provision

A large majority of early child education is publicly-provided—almost entirely by municipalities, but occasionally by states or by the federal government.[11] In 2009, 66 percent of children enrolled in creche and 76 percent of children in pre-school attended public institutions. These numbers are up from their 2001 levels of 62 percent and 75 percent, respectively—likely due to increased funding available through FUNDEB. Of course, these are the proportions of children accessing public institutions *among those* who are accessing ECE at all. A number of children attend unregistered institutions, as discussed in the next section. Children using informal or other unregistered care are not captured by these statistics, so they are likely overestimates of public provision in the education of under-five children.

Private early child education institutions are of two types: either entirely private, or publicly-funded and privately-owned and operated according to the stipulations of a contract with the municipal or state government (contracted, or "conveniada"). Examining the number of institutions in 2009, public creches and pre-schools were more common than private ones in every region of the country. Private creches and pre-schools are least common in the North and the Northeast—the two regions with the lowest per capita income—and most common in the Southeast, as shown in figure 3.18 and in figure 3.19.

Among private institutions, fully-private schools are more common than conveniada (contracted) private schools in each region and for both levels of ECE. The results of the next chapter show that conveniada creches and pre-schools have higher quality infrastructure than public schools. If public-private partnerships can provide higher quality care and education at equal or lower cost, then municipalities might consider expanding the use of this modality.

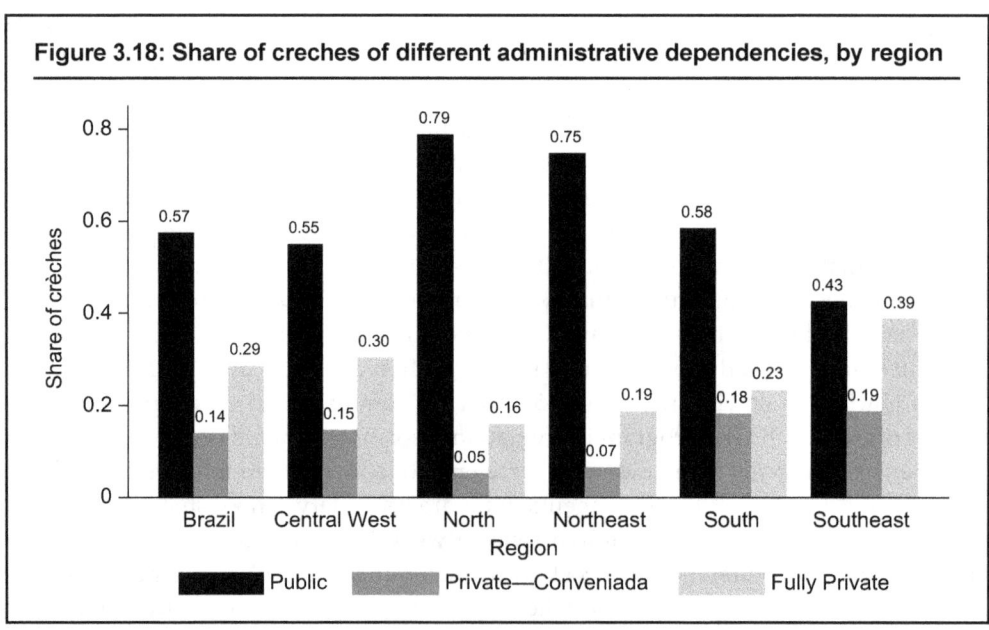

Figure 3.18: Share of creches of different administrative dependencies, by region

Source: Censo Escolar (2009).

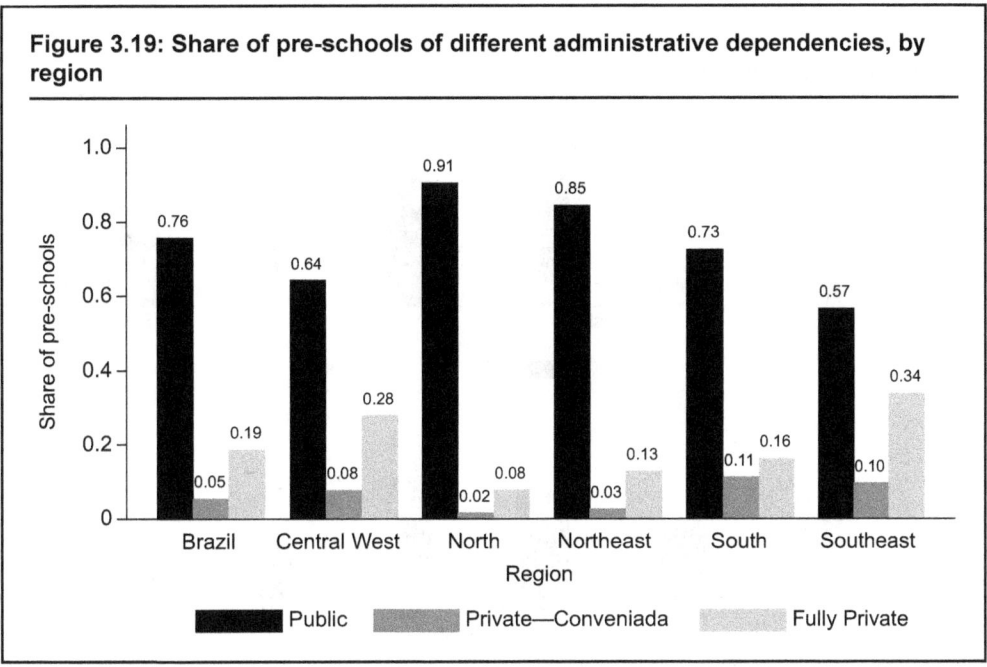

Figure 3.19: Share of pre-schools of different administrative dependencies, by region

Source: Censo Escolar (2009).

Unregistered institutions

Municipal governments only receive education funds—such as transfers coming through FUNDEF or FUNDEB—if they officially register their schools and participate in the Ministry of Education's annual Census of Schools. The Census of Schools gathers detailed data on students, teachers, and infrastructure in public and private educational institutions. However, there may be private institutions that are insufficiently incentivized to register or to respond to the Census of Schools. Unregistered institutions cannot be regulated and overseen by municipal governments. Also, when governments lack basic enrollment and school quality information, it is harder to plan ECE investments.

Household survey data reveal a much higher fraction of children enrolled in ECE than is captured in Census of Schools numbers. This discrepancy suggests that many children are involved in activities that their parents report as ECE, but which do not take place in officially registered ECE institutions. These might include "home creches," in which a neighborhood woman opens her home and provides care to a small group of children. Simple comparisons from the two data sources suggest that over one-third of pre-school students fit this description, as do as many as 12 percent of children enrolled in creche.

The fraction of children in unregistered creches fell dramatically during 2001–2009, from 34 percent to 12 percent (figure 3.20). This is likely due to incentives for municipalities to contract private creches to receive FUNDEB resources. Pre-school students, on the contrary, were about as likely to be in unregistered institutions in 2001 as in 2009.

Financing

Expanding the supply of creches and pre-schools and increasing enrollment in center-based ECE will require large amounts of additional funding over the coming years. This funding responsibility will fall most directly on municipal governments, as they are the

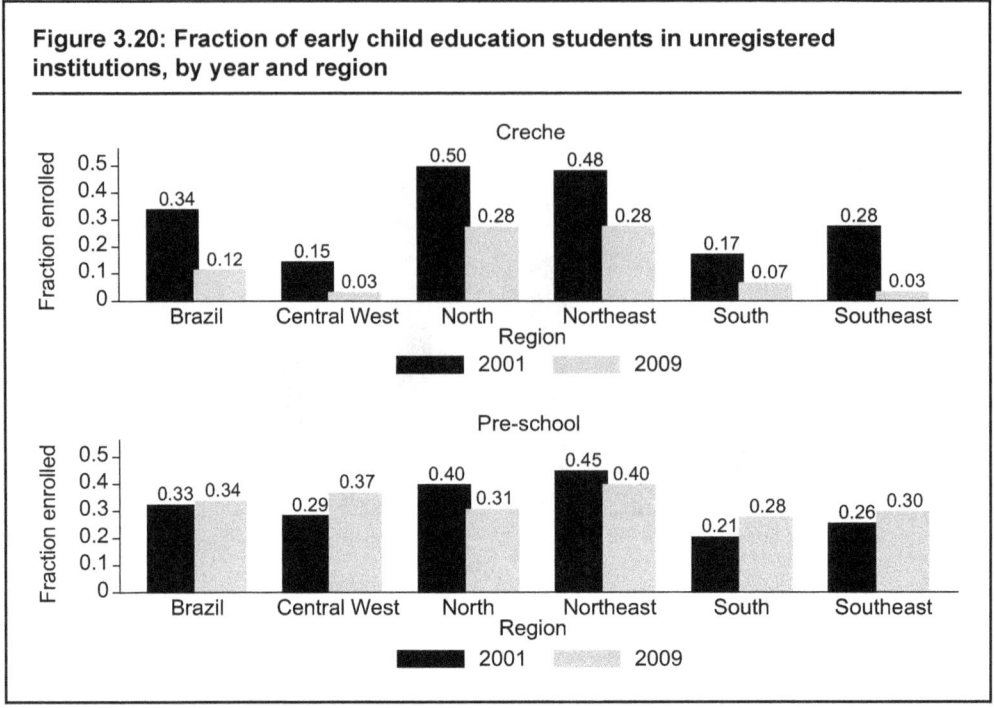

Figure 3.20: Fraction of early child education students in unregistered institutions, by year and region

Source: Censo Escolar (2001, 2009) and PNAD (2001, 2009).

primary providers of early child education. Given the unmet demand for creches and pre-schools, and the FUNDEB transfers to municipalities for each child they enroll in early child education, most municipalities will have incentives to further expand ECE. The federal government created additional incentives for investments in pre-school by making pre-school education compulsory as of 2009, although municipalities have until 2016 to reach full compliance.

Municipal governments have primary responsibility over early child education (ages 0–5) and primary and lower secondary education (ages 6–14).[12] Higher levels are handled by state and federal governments. Municipalities must spend at least 25 percent of revenue on education, but otherwise have remarkable policy autonomy and discretion. This has led to huge cross-municipality variation in early child education investment. Many municipal characteristics influence this variation, some of which are explored in Chapter Four.

Over 95 percent of public ECE financing is disbursed by municipal governments, although much of that expenditure comes from transfer revenues received from the state and federal governments.[13] Total municipal expenditure on early child education in 2009 totaled over 9.7 billion reais (US$5.7 billion). After municipalities pay a fixed share of revenue into a state-level FUNDEB fund, that fund is redistributed among municipalities in the state according to their share of enrolled public school students (with students at different grades weighted differently). In states where this redistribution does not reach an annually-set federal guaranteed minimum, the federal government agrees to top off the fund receipt. As of 2010, this meant that municipalities were guaranteed to receive at least R$1,558 (US$873) for each child enrolled in a public full-day creche (R$1,133 for partial day), and R$1,770 (US$912) for each child in a public full-day pre-school (R$1,416 for partial day). Municipalities in relatively rich states receive more, but no municipality receives less from the state fund.[14] Importantly, under FUNDEB, the only action municipalities can take to appreciably increase the receipts from the school fund is to increase the number of children enrolled in early child education.

Table 3.8: Annual municipal early child education expenditures in 2009, by region

Region	Total municipal creche and pre-school students	Total municipal expenditure on early child education	Municipal expenditure per enrolled early child education student (total reais)
North	504,089	281 million	558
Northeast	1,674,525	721 million	430
Southeast	2,364,619	6.83 billion	2,889
South	713,868	1.59 billion	2,228
Central West	305,158	297 million	974

Sources: Census of Schools (2009) and Tesouro Nacional Finbra Database (2009).

Municipal expenditure per child enrolled in early child education varies greatly across regions, as shown in table 3.8.[15] Cross-regional differences in per pupil expenditures are likely an important factor explaining differences in infrastructure quality, teacher training, and average class size. Dramatically, the Southeast spends 6.7 times more per enrolled public ECE child than does the relatively poor Northeast. While hiring teachers and building school infrastructure may be less costly in poorer regions of the country than in richer ones, this alone can only be a small part of the explanation: Different regions are clearly choosing different quantity-quality tradeoffs.

The share of total municipal education spending going to early child education has increased slightly in recent years, from a national average of 8.3 percent in 2004 to 9.3 percent in 2008. However, relative expenditure on early child education in the total education budget varies greatly across regions. In 2008, it was 3.2 percent in the North, 3.4 percent in the Northeast, 6.7 percent in the Central West, 12.3 percent in the South, and 14.8 percent in the Southeast.

Comparing these actual per-child ECE expenditures at the municipal level with FUNDEB transfers is revealing. It suggests that in the North, Northeast, and Central West, the average municipality spends less on each child enrolled in ECE than it obtains for enrolling that child. In those areas, FUNDEB should effectively remove the financial impediments poor municipalities might otherwise face to expanding early child education in response to demand, since FUNDEB provides more than the current expenditure per child for creche or pre-school. However, municipalities must also remove additional barriers to building and filling schools, such as by engaging in dialogue with parents about their needs.

The 2009 expenditures by region (table 3.8), combined with the number of children not enrolled in pre-school (table 3.2), provides a back-of-the-envelope calculation of the additional operating cost if Brazil were to enroll its 1,570,512 pre-school aged children that are currently not enrolled. The bill would come to about 2.6 billion reais, or US$1.6 billion. Brazil's total 2009 expenditures on ECE came to US$5.75 billion, so this would involve almost a 30 percent increase in the ECE bill, only including municipal expenditures (which are the great majority), and without any expansion in coverage for children age 0–3. Some of this expense will be off-set by the reduction in enrollments due to falling fertility, as well as by increased tax revenues from expanded female labor force participation. But achieving universal pre-school enrollment will still involve significant trade-offs.

Making quantity-quality trade-offs

Expanding enrollment in early child education and increasing its quality are twin goals, but they are also potentially competing spending priorities. Municipal governments must prioritize investments in order to grant access to previously-marginalized children (especially the poor and disadvantaged) without sacrificing the quality needed to make early child education worthwhile.

Because pre-school has become a compulsory level of education, there is no longer a substantive quantity-quality trade-off. That is, sacrificing quantity for the sake of quality is no longer an option. The goal of municipalities is to maintain quality in the face of enrollment expansion, and to make new investments in those aspects of quality that deliver the highest returns. The trade-off being made is between various different types of potential investment in quality. The evidence presented in Chapter Two suggests some particularly high-return investments; specifically, investment in the quality of activities and in program structure. Exchanging investments in other aspects of quality—such as in the general education level of teachers—for these high-return investments is likely a good strategy.

Creche education is not compulsory, which introduces a stark quantity-quality trade-off. For example, the fact that the Northeast region spends less per child on early child education than does the North or the Central West, and yet has a higher creche enrollment rate than does either, suggests this trade-off. Local priorities determine the choices made by each municipality. It is instructive to examine what it would cost to meet estimated unmet demand for creche spaces (table 3.4), assuming that new creche spaces have the same "average quality" as existing creche spaces. Alternatively, one can compute how many fewer children would be granted access if the same amount of money were spent, but if the quality of new creche spaces were increased.

The 2009 expenditures by region (table 3.8), combined with the estimated unmet demand for creche spaces (table 3.4) provides a back-of-the-envelope calculation of the additional operating cost if Brazil were to enroll the almost 1.8 million children nationwide who are not enrolled but whose parents would want them enrolled in a creche. The bill would come to about 2.6 billion reais (US$1.6 billion). This is almost the same amount of money that would be required to enroll all not enrolled 4–5 year olds in pre-school. Brazil's total 2009 expenditures on ECE came to US$5.75 billion, so this expansion in creche enrollment would also involve almost a 30 percent increase in the ECE bill, only including municipal expenditures (which are the great majority).

Alternatively, Barros et al. (2011a) imply that a 6 percent increase in creche expenditures dedicated to improvements in the quality of activities and in program structure would increase a child's development age by a sizeable 3.5 months, which is a full 0.5 standard deviation improvement in overall development. This implies that for the same 2.6 billion Reais that could satisfy all unmet demand for creche at the current average quality level of creches, one could enroll over 1.6 million children (94 percent of unmet demand) at a quality level that implies an additional 3.5 months of development for each of these children. Of course, that increase in quality would mean that some unmet demand (about 6 percent) for creche would *remain* unmet, and these children would not get any of the benefits of creche attendance. Given the returns in child development to improvements in quality, it is highly likely that those quality improvements outweigh the benefits of offering lower quality creche care to all children who desire creche care.[16] Thus, meeting all unmet demand—at the expense of creche quality—may be a poor investment.

Lessons

Brazil has made great strides in the provision of early child education in recent years. However, there is a significant gap to fill, both in rural and urban areas, to achieve universal pre-school education by 2016 and to provide creche services to needy children throughout the country. To achieve this, municipalities must be strategic in the construction of new pre-schools and creches, and must use poverty and population data to identify the areas of greatest need. In extremely rural areas, the government will also need to explore alternative delivery mechanisms whenever the transportation of young children is sufficiently complicated to make center-based care unrealistic. While there are alternatives to center-based early child cognitive stimulation in place in a few locales, Brazil can facilitate further exploration by setting clear minimum standards and permitting municipalities to investigate the possibilities. Finally, given the significant costs associated with expanding access to early child education, municipalities must set clear priorities and make quantity-quality trade-offs that will efficiently achieve those priorities. At the level of creche education—which need not be universal—municipalities may find that improvements in the quality of activities and in program structure for creches that service the most disadvantaged children yield more benefits than does expanding the number of available spaces in existing public creches.

Notes

1. Before 2004, the Pesquisa Nacional por Amostra de Domicilios (PNAD) did not survey urban parts of six of the seven states in the North (Rondônia, Acre, Amazonas, Roraima, Pará, and Amapá). As a result, data for the North is not representative of the entire region until 2004, and the North is not shown in this or other figures until 2004.
2. The trends are similar if one examines the pre-school enrollment rate of only children ages 4–5. For consistency over time, enrollment is reported for children ages 4–6 unless specified otherwise.
3. Regressions at the state aggregate and child levels suggest that this gap and its divergence over time are statistically significant. Specifically, regressing creche attendance on mother's working status, year dummy variables, and their interactions suggests that a mother's participation in the labor force has a significant, positive effect on creche attendance that is increasing over time. The same thing can be shown by using a time trend in place of year dummy variables; once again, the coefficient on mother's working status is significant and positive, as is the interaction term.
4. This report uses the São Paulo state average pre-school size of 87 students per school.
5. Federal Constitution of 1988, Title 8, Chapter 3, Section 1, Art 208, Proposition 4.
6. The National Network for Early Childhood is a voluntary network made up of government agencies (the Ministries of Education, Health, and Social Development), international nonprofits working in Brazil (e.g., Plan International, Promundo), and a host of local nonprofits and private sector representatives, with 86 member organizations altogether. These organizations are joined in dialogue to improve national policies related to children age zero to six years.

7. Of course, income may be more highly correlated with urbanization in some regions compared to others. In a region where rich families are more likely to live in urban areas than are poor families, and where demand for creche care is lower in rural areas, then these estimates of demand may be too large.

8. The lottery is further detailed in Appendix C.

9. The study cannot rule out that EDIs are also concentrated in municipalities with particular interest in early child education. However, the study did control for various characteristics of the educational institution, reducing some of that potential bias.

10. "Florestania" is a new word that has been defined as "citizenship of the forest," used to describe a pragmatic philosophy of sustainable environmentally friendly development, coined by the State of Acre's Jorge Viana administration.

11. As of 2009, only about 1.7 percent of all public creche and pre-school students were in state and federal schools.

12. Municipal governments provide most public primary education (83 percent of students in 2007), but the state government has primary schools in some municipalities.

13. The exact amount is impossible to calculate given that FUNDEB transfers are not broken down by levels of education. However, 88.7 percent of total municipal revenues come from transfers (2008), and as education is one of the sectors most targeted by inter-government transfer programs (i.e., FUNDEB), the number for education is probably even higher.

14. The federal government ensures per-student minima by 'topping off' those state funds whose per students amounts fall below the federally-chosen minima.

15. These include both operating and construction costs.

16. In the quality improvement scenario, the quality improvements would lead to 3.5 months of additional development per child times more than 1.6 million children, which implies almost 6 million collective months of additional development. This is a substantial increase. For it to be a better choice to enroll all unmet demand at existing creche quality levels than to enroll only 94 percent of unmet demand at a higher level of creche quality, one would have to believe that the 100,000 children excluded by the latter policy would each earn over 58 months (almost 5 years) of additional development by attending a creche, as opposed to staying at home. This seems highly unlikely.

CHAPTER 4

The Next Steps for Brazil's Children

Brazil has made important strides in extending access to Early Child Education. The road ahead is long but if Brazil is pro-active and prudent in its targeting, it can ensure ECE opportunities for its most vulnerable children in the medium-run and—over time—for all its children. Quality of early child education is also improving along some dimensions, albeit with significant room for improvement. Beyond these two fundamental missions of expanding coverage and improving quality, what are the next steps to ensure healthy early child development for Brazil's youngest?

This chapter explores three innovative areas with the potential to improve early child development in Brazil: cross-sectoral collaboration, leveraging private sector resources in a way that improves provision, quality, and innovation in early child education, and safeguarding opportunities for children in municipalities with less political will for service delivery.

Cross-Sectoral Collaboration

Coordinated early child development programs, both at the policy level and at the program or service-delivery level, have the potential to deliver greater benefits and to reduce costs relative to efforts in individual sectors (such as education, health, or social assistance). Several countries have made great strides in coordinating policies as well as combining service delivery. Brazil has recently made strong steps in the direction of coordinated policy, through the National Plan for Early Childhood, but there is much room for expanding and improving coordinated service delivery.

Complementarity

As discussed in Chapter One, interventions that combine education and nutrition tend to have more positive impacts on children's cognitive development than those that provide nutritional or financial transfers alone. In addition, programs often have strong effects outside the expected mechanisms. Studies have shown that school-based health programs also have large education impacts, as evidenced by a program to treat schoolchildren for intestinal worms in Kenya (Miguel and Kremer 2004) and in an iron supplementation program in Indian pre-schools (Bobonis, Miguel and Puri-Sharma 2006). Moreover, cash transfers can boost health outcomes in the same way that nutrition programs can (Nores and Barnett 2010).

Improved access to services

Multisectoral programs also allow parents to find information on and access all the services they need to help their children flourish in one place, rather than needing to separately seek out services about which they may be unaware. A study of comprehensive social assistance and care for families with young children, including health promotion, employment training for parents, and recreation activities for children, showed significant effects relative to non-comprehensive services that parents had to search for individually (Browne et al. 2001).

Cost savings

These programs also have the potential to generate significant cost savings. Delivering services for two sectors—e.g., education and health—at the same center or during the same home visit is much less costly than making separate visits. Yet these cross-sectoral programs do come at a cost: Government ministries are built to deliver services within sectors, and coordination can be challenging, both logistically and politically. Leaders in various states of Brazil have cited the challenges of seeking to coordinate across sectors for exactly these reasons. In several countries, and in some parts of Brazil, such cross-sectoral cooperation around early child development has been initiated. This cooperation has occurred at both the level of coordinating efforts (e.g., having a cross-sectoral plan for early child development) and at the level of coordinating programs (e.g., having joint programs that offer services in multiple sectors). Best practices from a number of other countries, as well as efforts within Brazil, can maximize the efficiency of future efforts.

Cross-sectoral collaboration in Brazil: The National Plan for Early Childhood

Brazil, through the National Network for Early Childhood, has developed a twelve-year National Plan for Early Childhood (Rede Nacional Primeira Infância 2010) (table 4.1). The document was prepared over the course of two years of deliberations and was launched in December 2010. This ambitious plan outlines thirteen goal areas, ranging from education, health, and social protection to confronting violence against children and protecting children from consumer pressure. In each area, a series of desired actions is presented. The plan then establishes five key instruments to achieve these goals, and actions therein.

The creation of this plan is an excellent step toward a cross-sectoral policy, complete with goals for different time periods over the next twelve years. In order to achieve even some of the gains proposed here, the Brazilian government will need to study, refine, and approve the plan. It will then need to create a coordinating group, like Jamaica's Early Childhood Commission, with key stakeholders and with a budget line, to oversee implementation in coordination with the many partners in early childhood.

The first step is underway, as the National Council of Children and Adolescents' Rights (CONANDA) approved the plan in December 2010. However, in order for the plan to have a true impact, the Government of Brazil will need to establish a coordinating agency to oversee its implementation. The experience of other countries in this area can guide Brazil's efforts. In several countries, overall ECD policy is housed in the Ministry of Education: this is the case in the United Kingdom, as well as in Sweden and in several developing countries, such as Nepal and Kenya. Jamaica has adopted a related but distinct approach by creating an explicitly cross-sectoral Early Childhood Commission: although it is housed within the Ministry of Education, the executive director of the commission is a physician. In Chile, the government adopted an alternative approach to coordinating its early childhood program, Chile Crece Contigo, by placing it in the Ministry of Planning to avoid sector identification (V. Silva 2010). Without an executing body with funding, the Brazil plan is likely to have the same fate as the ECE goals of the National Plan for Education for 2001 to 2010: the great majority of states and municipalities made no moves to provide resources to achieve the goals, the federal government did

Table 4.1: Brazil's National Plan for Early Childhood

Goal area	Example of associated action
Healthy children	Achieve six months of maternity leave in the public sector and encourage the same in the private sector
Early child education	In three years, ensure that all Early Child Education centers have formulated their pedagogical improvement plans and are in the process of implementation
Family and community of the child	Validate, by way of public policies of support, the family unit as the main locus of production of the child's basic social identity
Social assistance to children and their families	Achieve universal follow-up with families in Bolsa Familia that are not fulfilling established conditions, prioritizing families with children up to six years old
Children in vulnerable situations: foster system, foster families, adoption	Guarantee, within two years, the satisfaction of basic human resource norms in the Ministry of Social Development: 1 psychologist and 1 social worker for every 20 children
Right to play	Annual information campaigns about the importance of play
City and the environment	Legally mandate that new *loteamentos*[a] reserve dedicated spaces for social apparatus attending to children's rights to health, education, social assistance, and leisure
Diversity: Black children, indigenous children, and quilombola[b] children	Create new pre-service training courses for early childhood educators, specifically dealing with nuances of indigenous culture
Confronting violence against children	Campaigns to confront violence in early childhood
Assuring documentation of citizenship for all children	Take action so that in three years, every municipality has at least one *Cartório* (Registry Office for Naturalized Persons)
Protecting children from consumer pressure	Promote the prohibition or limitation of sale of unhealthy food in school canteens as well as advertising in schools
Controlling early exposure of children to media	Prohibit the presence of TVs in creches and regulate their use in pre-schools (only for teaching purposes)
Avoiding accidents in early childhood	Promote the creation and fulfillment of legislation intended to avoid poisonings caused by accidental ingestion of medication and cleaning products
Instruments to achieve these goals	
Training professionals for Early Childhood	Stimulate through incentive programs, create post-graduate courses relating to early child development
The role of social media	Mobilize states, the federal district, and the municipalities so that they develop their own plans for early child development
Legislative power	Provide ongoing and detailed support to the conversion of the National Plan for Child Development into law
Research on early childhood	Create incentives for research on early child development—for example, a committee and a budget line (in state organizations such as INEP, CNPq, etc.)
State & municipal plans for early childhood	Construct plans with ample social participation, subject to analysis and approval by the Executive Power; then submit them to the legislative body for analysis, refinement, and approval

Source: Rede Nacional Primeira Infância (2010).
Note: a. Loteamentos are subdivisions of land created for residential housing.
b. Quilombolas are communities principally populated by the descendants of slaves.

not maintain this as a focus, and the ECE coverage goal—particularly at the 0–3 level—was missed completely (Moço 2010).[1]

Other efforts to promote inter-sectoral coordination in Brazil include the ongoing development of a Unified Program of Integrated Care in Early Childhood by the federal-level Office of Strategic Action in the Secretariat for Strategic Affairs of the Presidency of Brazil, as well as efforts that take place at a more local level through information sharing. For example, various organizations—including the World Bank and the non-governmental organization Avante—have carried out mappings of early child services in different municipalities to, at the very least, inform each sector of the activities of other sectors. This information is a first and necessary step to coordination.

International experience in strategic ECD planning: Jamaica's
National Strategic Plan for Early Childhood Development

As with Brazil and its National Plan for Early Childhood, Jamaica in 2008 launched a five-year National Strategic Plan (NSP) for Early Childhood Development. The NSP was developed by the Early Childhood Commission and established by the Jamaican parliament in 2003 to ensure that children under age eight have access to high-quality social services. While housed within the Ministry of Education, the NSP coordinates services across the Ministries of Health, Labor, Finance, and the government agencies for technical and vocational education and for training, as well as a number of non-governmental partners. The NSP lays out five processes to improve early child development, as well as two processes to improve the effectiveness of the NSP itself. Each process has a set of related activities.[2]

In its first two years, the plan has had marked successes, demonstrating how a coordinated plan can improve ECD policy. These successes include approval of a Standards and Accreditation System for early childhood parenting education and support programs, development of a curriculum and delivery model for child development therapy, complete initial inspection of 35 percent of Early Child Institutions, and the design, development, and implementation of a management information system for ECD (JIS News 2010).

While the Jamaican National Strategic Plan has led to advances, it has also faced challenges. Because the plan was largely developed by a small group, buy-in from some service providers has been limited, leading to bottlenecks in the implementation of some of the goal activities. Furthermore, communication and coordination among members of the executive committee have been hampered by inter-personal conflicts, highlighting the importance of selecting leadership for an executing body with a cross-sectoral background and strong management and diplomatic skills. Brazil's national plan was developed in an extensively collaborative process over a long period of time, but if—upon legalization—the government goes on to create a coordinating body, appointing the right staff for this will be critical to avoiding impediments in implementation.

International experience in cross-sectoral service delivery: Chile Crece Contigo

In addition to comprehensive ECD plans, several countries have had success with service delivery that cuts across sectors, providing education, health, and other services from one point of contact. International examples include Chile's program, *Chile Crece Contigo* (Chile Grows With You, or ChCC), New Zealand's Family Start and Well Child Tamariki Ora Service, and England's Sure Start program.

ChCC's coordinated program can inform similar goals in Brazil. In 2005, the Chilean government organized an inter-ministerial working group, coordinated by the Ministry of Planning, which included the Ministries of Health and Education as well as the Budget Office. They spent one year carrying out a range of studies to (a) categorize the existing programs related to early childhood, including small-scale programs, (b) explore key issues not previously studied, (c) ascertain Chilean perceptions of early child development, and (d) update statistics, indicators, and results related to early childhood in Chile. In 2006, they prepared a proposal of government measures needed to create a system for integrated protection of early childhood. In 2007 they created the program, and in 2009 the system was integrated into law. ChCC provides comprehensive care to children from pre-natal care for mothers until the children enter pre-school (at four or five years old) (table 4.2).

Table 4.2: Services offered under Chile Crece Contigo

Target Group	Services
All children	1. Mass Education Program 2. Interactive information spaces 3. Proposals for improved legislation
Children who participate in the public health system	4. Biopsychological development support program
Vulnerable children	5. Home visits by health team 6. Automatic access to family subsidy 7. Access to free, high quality nurseries and childcare 8. Preferential access to public programs 9. Integrated attention to children with delays 10. Technical assistance for children with disabilities

Source: Adapted from Silva (2010).

One valuable lesson from ChCC is that coordinating the policy in a non-sectoral ministry (e.g., planning rather than health or education), can be advantageous both for more efficient management of loans and grants, and to minimize cross-sectoral territorial issues. A second lesson is that the sum of cross-sectoral early child development coordination has the potential to be much more than the sum of its component sectors. The coordination in ChCC had led not only to increased investment in each area, but also to investments across sectors. For example, children with a developmental delay identified in the first few months are referred to a "stimulation room" (*sala de estimulación*), where they and their parents receive one-on-one or group attention in cognitive and motor stimulation, employing many of the same skills and exercises used in childcare centers and pre-schools. Rather than merely having larger education and health investments for early childhood, children are now accessing educational interventions within the health sector, providing cognitive stimulation to more young children in need. ChCC also relies on an integrated monitoring system, wherein a subset of the data from health and education programs feeds into a single system that sends notifications for intervention when the data predict a concern for the child. Such a system is another advantage of an integrated program like ChCC.

Center-based cross-sectoral programs

Integrated child development programs exist around the world, in both the public and nonprofit sectors. Some of these programs provide center-based services, some provide home-based services, and many provide a mix, wherein home-based services take place after a referral from the health or education sector (as is the case with Chile Crece Contigo). New Zealand's "Well Child Tamariki Ora Services" program is an example of a well-developed, center-based program that provides comprehensive health care for children ages 0–5, in addition to parent training and information. Likewise, the Swedish pre-school system provides free pre-school for children from age one to five. The health sector works closely with the pre-schools so that screenings for attention deficits, hearing problems, and motor delays are all available at the center (Matthews 2010).

Movement toward service delivery coordination in Brazil

The most established example of cross-sectoral collaboration in early child development in Brazil is the Rio Grande do Sul program Primeira Infância Melhor, described in some detail in Chapter Two. Although the program is housed in the State Health

Secretariat, it is managed by the State Technical Group, which includes technical staff from the Secretariats of Health, Education, Culture, Justice, and Social Development, regional coordinators from health and education from across the state, and others. At the municipal level, the program is run by the Municipal Technical Group, which also includes representatives from all participating secretariats. This local group runs the program completely, from organizing and monitoring activities to providing training to the field workers (Schneider and Ramires 2007).

The Education Secretariat of the state of Acre sends educational agents into the homes of rural children twice weekly to provide cognitive stimulation. It is working with the Health Secretariat to coordinate both educational visits and diagnostic information collection so that children receive the highest possible quality of services. Municipalities are also seeking to coordinate services: the Education Secretariat of Rio de Janeiro municipality is currently endeavoring to bring health professionals into each creche to ensure that children have access to health services while at an education center.

These programs are breaking ground, but increased coordination and cooperation across sectors to deliver services to children will make it possible for more children to receive the range of services they need, at lower cost and to greater effect.

Leveraging Private Sector Provision, Funding, and Innovation

Given the massive expansion in ECE required over the coming years and the likely budget implications of achieving coverage and quality goals, the private sector may be a critical resource for providing care and education. Private investment and innovation in early child education could effectively complement public funding—especially if public construction and expansion is slow to materialize and meet growing demand.

Provision

The most recent data show that more than one third of creche spaces are provided by the private sector: 29 percent are fully private and 14 percent are *conveniado* (or government contracted). Likewise, at the pre-school level, a quarter of provision is through the private sector: 19 percent fully private and 5 percent conveniado. Private provision is growing rapidly, with hundreds of early child education institutions contracted each year (M. d. Silva 2010). The expansion signals significant capacity in the private sector to supplement the efforts of the public sector in providing early child services. Furthermore, data on quality suggest that contracted institutions have better infrastructure, on average, than do public institutions. Brazil's Ministry of Education has published a guide to assist municipalities in the development of *conveniado* relationships which may help municipalities expand the use of this modality to provide ECE (MEC 2009).

Given the potential capacity of the private sector and the desired expansion, Brazil may need to leverage non-public providers. Other countries that have expanded rapidly have had to do so. The Head Start pre-school program in the United States, which has expanded by as much as 50,000 spaces in a single year and now serves 900,000 pre-school children, relies exclusively on contracted centers similar to *conveniados* (OHS 2010). In contrast, during 2001–2005, Mexico expanded ECE for 3–5 year-olds by over one million spaces, almost entirely through the public system. However, this included major increases in class size—in many cases to over 30 students per caregiver (Yoshikawa et al. 2007). Private investment might be useful in avoiding such deteriorations in quality.

Although FUNDEB reimbursements are equal for public and *conveniado* spaces, municipalities have the liberty to compensate *conveniado* spaces at either higher or lower levels, providing the freedom to create incentives for private provision for difficult-to-reach populations (MEC 2009). Two international examples of this strategy to reach difficult populations come from the United States and Chile. A recent revision of the U.S. Head Start policy created a range of special incentives for programs to reach homeless children (NAEHCY 2008), who are likely the hardest-to-reach and hardest-to-serve population in the United States.

Similarly, the Chilean government included pre-kindergarten and kindergarten in its Preferential School Subsidy program in 2008, which provides additional resources to early child and primary education institutions that cater to the most vulnerable children. In Chile, the vulnerable children are identified either because they are enrolled in Chile's main social transfer program (Chile Solidario), because they are in the bottom third of vulnerability according to the social protection register (comparable to Brazil's *cadastro único*), because they are in the public health program, or—finally—because they are not in those programs but are still in low-income households (MINED 2011). Institutions receive additional resources per vulnerable child reached as well as for enrolling higher concentrations of vulnerable children. The program also includes incentives to encourage schools to use the additional resources to improve opportunities for the most vulnerable children: schools receive some of the monetary incentives upon enrollment and the rest upon approval of their plan to improve education for vulnerable populations. Likewise in Brazil, municipalities can experiment with ways to provide additional incentives to reach the most difficult-to-reach children, and MEC can develop guidelines to reach these children, leveraging the innovation of the private sector.

Private sector funding

In addition to subsidized provision through the private sector, expanding public-private partnerships may offset some of the budget impacts of expanding coverage and improving the quality of Brazil's ECE. Businesses can realize short-term benefits from investments in early child development in terms of reduced employee absenteeism and turnover due to child care problems. Indeed, in the United States and elsewhere, productivity and reduced absenteeism have both been clearly linked to quality child care (Shellenback 2004, Anderson 2009). In addition, the private sector—from a longer-term viewpoint—benefits from a well-educated and well-developed workforce, for which early child development is an essential ingredient.

Many corporations have a philanthropic arm which can contribute to ECD, and a number of corporations across Brazil are doing this. In many countries, these corporate donations are mobilized as matching funds to provide and improve ECD services. A recent review of ECD partnerships in the United States revealed some common characteristics for success. They tend to pool funds from public, private, and nonprofit coffers and channel them through a state or local central nonprofit with a particular early child mandate. The focus of these partnerships has been on expanding pre-school, developing both in-home and out-of-home early child education opportunities, and—most commonly—creating integrated, cross-sectoral early child development systems (as discussed earlier in this chapter). Several partnerships also promote best practices, facilitating the cross-municipal learning discussed in the previous chapter (NGA 2008). These partnerships can be formed wherever there is the will, and a series of steps (outlined in table 4.3) has been successful in leading to their creation.

Table 4.3: Steps to establishing public-private partnerships for ECD

1. Convene leaders from the public, private, and nonprofit sectors to highlight the importance of ECD and make a call to action
2. Identity resources from each group (financial, human, and in-kind) that can form the basis of a partnership
3. Formalize government commitment through legislation of an executing body
4. Determine the executing body's governance structure
5. Develop an evaluation strategy

Source: Adapted from NGA (2008). Steps are derived from partnerships in the United States.

In Brazil, an example of public-private cooperation is the Millenium Fund for Early Childhood Education, which promotes in-service training and capacity building for staff and administrators of early child education centers in 15 municipalities of southern Brazil (Paiva et al. 2009). One specific initiative is the creation of "Education Boards," a physical space in which early child educators receive training through hands-on participation in the same kinds of play-based activities that they should share with children. In this partnership, municipal education secretariats provide instruction to trainers, UNESCO provides office space for coordinating the program, and private sector donors—principally the Gerdau Institute, among others—provide funding for the program's operating costs and materials. As Brazil seeks to attain lofty coverage goals for both creche and pre-school, these kinds of partnerships may prove critical to expanding capacity.

Public-private partnerships also provide opportunities to innovate, as private funds can be leveraged to experiment with new modalities and delivery mechanisms for which public funds may incite controversy. An example from primary education is the introduction of pay-for-performance for students in New York City, which met with criticism but was politically defensible since privately-donated funds were used for the pilot transfers. Many existing public-private partnerships outside Brazil provide grants to localities to improve ECD, allowing creativity in the exact application of resources (NGA 2008). In New Zealand, the Centers of Innovation program provides grants to ECE centers to innovate and evaluate, experimenting with new pedagogies, integration of families with center care, and other areas (Gibbs and Poskitt 2009).

Compensating for Differences across Municipalities

The Constitution affords extensive municipal government autonomy over early child education policy, which has led to huge variation in investment. Many municipal characteristics influence this variation, including the wealth of the average citizen and the degree of inequality in the income distribution (demonstrated by Kosec 2011). In planning national early child education policy, the federal government should take into account how different municipalities are differently motivated to expand ECE. This will help the government develop policies that create incentives for investment where it is needed most.

Of course, investment in early child education may be limited by the availability of public funds. When public funds are low, early child education—and especially creche education, still not compulsory—may be viewed as a dispensable luxury good when compared with compulsory pre-school and primary education. However, following the FUNDEF and FUNDEB school finance equalization reforms, the amount of revenue available for education has become less tied to a municipality's economic level. By redistributing revenue within states, from rich to poor municipalities, these reforms have facilitated ECE investment in precisely those areas where research suggests it will have the greatest impact: poor municipalities.

Income, inequality, and ECE investment

Shifting funds between different municipalities is important since not all municipalities have the same incentives to invest additional revenue in early child education. In a study of Brazil's over 5,000 municipalities during 1995–2008 (the period during which FUNDEF and FUNDEB were enacted), Kosec (2011) demonstrates two key points about municipal characteristics and ECE investment. First, public creches and pre-schools do not benefit all citizens equally. They disproportionately benefit poorer citizens, since the poor are the most likely to use these public services. Rich families tend to enroll their children in private school, and therefore are less invested in the public education system. Second, the distribution of income in a municipality hugely affects public early child education investment. Given extra revenue (such as that provided by FUNDEB), poor and equal municipalities are more likely to expand early child education than are richer and more unequal municipalities. They are especially likely to expand ECE if they have participatory budgeting policies in place, which allow citizens in each neighborhood to directly vote on how their neighborhood will spend a share of municipal funds.

Kosec's results are easily illustrated by comparing a group of pre-school age children not enrolled in school that live in a municipality with median inequality (Gini coefficient of 0.39) with similar groups of children in municipalities with lower and higher inequality. If the municipality with median inequality is given enough new revenue to expand ECE and enroll 100 new children, more unequal municipalities given the same amount of money will enroll fewer than 100 children, and more equal municipalities will enroll more than 100 children, as illustrated in figure 4.1. Likewise, if the municipality with median income is given enough new revenue to expand ECE and enroll 100

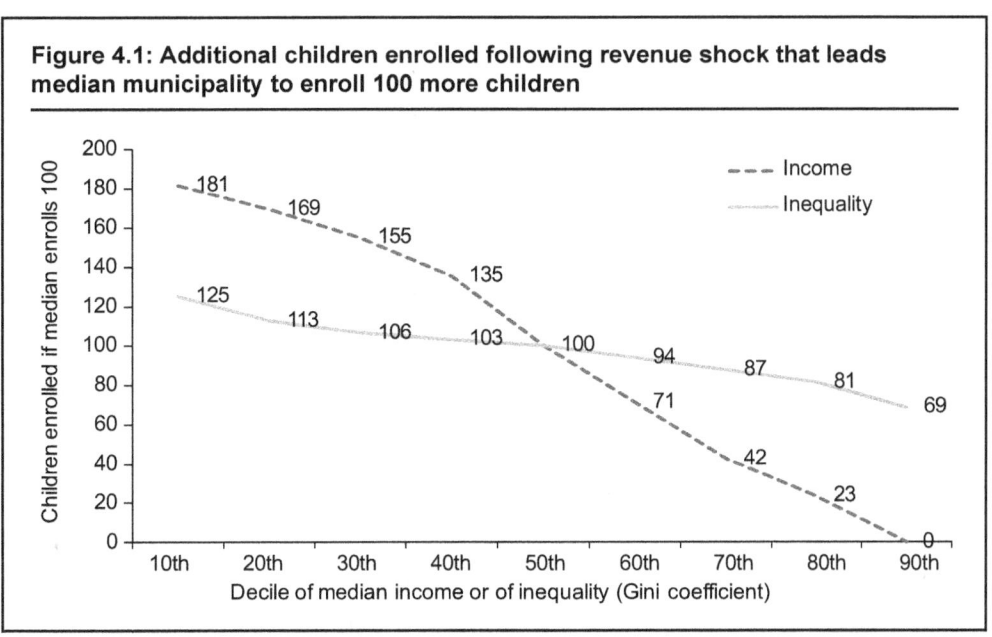

Figure 4.1: Additional children enrolled following revenue shock that leads median municipality to enroll 100 more children

Source: Kosec (2011), using data from Censo Escolar (1995–2008), Tesouro Nacional (1995–2008), and IBGE Censo (2000).

new children, richer municipalities given the same amount of money will enroll fewer than 100 children, and poorer municipalities will enroll more than 100 children. Poorer municipalities are more likely to enroll new children given any amount of additional revenue. Income appears to matter more than inequality in determining how likely a municipality is to put extra revenue into expanding early child education.

Policy implications

These findings have at least two important policy implications. First, revenue transfers that target the poorest and least unequal municipalities are likely to be the most effective in expanding early child education. Policy makers in those municipalities already have a relatively strong desire to spend their next Reais of revenue on early child education. Targeting funds at those municipalities means the money is more likely to end up in early child education. In richer and more unequal municipalities, a transfer of funds is more likely to end up in public primary or lower-secondary education, or in goods other than education, like public infrastructure. If the goal is to expand public early child education, then federally-imposed minimum spending or universal provision requirements may be necessary in municipalities with high income inequality.

A corollary of this point is that FUNDEB would create better incentives for investment in early child education if it involved national redistribution rather than within-state redistribution. A national redistribution would ensure that Brazil's poorest municipalities receive the largest influxes of money under FUNDEB, and that its richest municipalities receive the smallest. At present, a poor municipality located in an even poorer state seems rich relative to other municipalities in that state, and therefore loses money through FUNDEB. At the same time, some rich municipalities (in the nation-wide sense) that are poor relative to other municipalities in their state are gaining money. A nation-wide redistribution program would eliminate these imbalances and ensure that money intended to expand public education goes to those municipalities most likely to make these investments. There may be political stumbling blocks to such a policy change, given the strength of state governors and representatives in federal policymaking. However, such a policy would be a substantial step in the direction of evening the playing field across states and not only within them.

Second, these results suggest that improving governance can significantly boost investment in early child education. Increasing the transparency and accountability of local government and enacting participatory budgeting are viable solutions to low investment that do not require externally imposing minimum expenditures or increasing the budget. These changes work by ensuring that the poor—who have the highest demand for public ECE but are often socially and politically marginalized—are more directly and fully involved in decision-making. The federal and state governments could increase public ECE investment by encouraging municipalities to make their budgets and expenditures transparent, and by encouraging them to explore ways to give poor citizens a voice in local government. Incentives that encourage participatory budgeting in particular may be effective in expanding early child education.

The potential power of participatory budgeting

Participatory budgeting (PB) has been shown to make a rich or unequal municipality more likely to convert extra revenue into early child education spending. But what exactly is PB, and how can governments bring it about? Following Brazil's return to democracy in 1985, many municipalities implemented PB. Under PB, citizens vote on how to use a share of municipal revenue designated for their neighborhood, and they elect neighborhood representatives to make municipality-wide spending decisions. Citizens deliberate and negotiate over the distribution of public resources. Policy makers publicize budgets and expenditures to promote transparency. Case studies from Brazil suggest that PB increases participation of marginalized groups, leads to more pro-poor expenditures, and increases government accountability (Souza 2001). Empirical evidence suggests that Brazilian municipalities with PB spend a slightly larger share of their budgets on health and education programs (Boulding and Wampler 2010). By dividing the budget into tracts assigned to each neighborhood, PB mechanically ensures a relatively equal distribution of political power. Thus, resulting policies are more likely to reflect the will of the people and not only that of the most politically powerful citizens.

In Brazil, PB has typically been implemented under a situation of divided government, where the municipal mayor and the municipal legislative council are pursuing two separate political agendas (Melo 2009). The legislative council can veto any budget, but it is politically difficult to do so when the budget comes from the people through PB. When divided government paralyzes policymaking, mayors implement PB to get the policy process moving again. More often than not, PB has remained in place once initially introduced. If PB simultaneously promises to politically empower otherwise marginalized citizens while also increasing spending on early child education, then the federal government may wish to create incentives for and encourage PB as part of a broader ECE development policy. The government could even incentivize more limited forms of PB that specifically apply only to spending on education.

Lessons

Cross-sectoral collaboration

Coordination and multisectoral provision of services provide an opportunity to make good programs even better, to ensure that parents receive the full array of services that their children need, and to reduce costs by offering services at a single location. Of course, integrating early child development services is not a panacea. An important example in the United States is the Comprehensive Child Development Program, which employed case management and home visiting to ensure that low-income children received health, education, and social assistance services. A large evaluation of the program found no average impact whatsoever (St. Pierre and Layzer 1999).[3] Coordinated services cannot compensate for poor quality education, health, or social assistance programs. However, as the government of Brazil seeks to improve quality in early child education and in other services, cross-sectoral coordination will be key to ensuring that quality.

In Brazil, integrating health services into creches to provide more opportunities to identify developmental delays and health problems and to provide services for those children early on will lead to significant improvements in child welfare. However, in every country where inter-sectoral coordination has been effective, it has required both strong national and local leadership. Because this coordination requires moving outside standard secretariats of health and education, establishing a cross-sectoral coordinating agency and encouraging integration of services can go a long way toward ensuring that children receive the help they need to contribute to Brazil's future growth.

Public-private partnerships

Partnerships outside the public sector can provide significant resources to expand ECD services, improve the quality thereof, and innovate in reaching the most vulnerable populations. Municipalities should engage the private sector to innovate on the quality of services and explore the possibility of using private sector providers to reach the most difficult-to-reach populations in innovative ways. MEC can identify and highlight best-practice examples of public-private partnerships.

Compensating for municipal differences

Even as educational financing reforms, especially FUNDEB, have created new incentives to invest in early child education, these incentives are distributed unequally, with poor children in richer and more unequal municipalities receiving fewer services. Elements of participatory budgeting processes can protect the poorest children even in these municipalities and have received positive feedback in the past. MEC can provide guidance to municipalities and states as to how to implement elements of PB policies to protect the poorest children.

Notes

1. The pre-school goal was almost attained.
2. These are laid out in detail in Appendix H.
3. Later research revealed that the program was effective *for certain sub-groups* (Ryan et al. 2002).

Appendixes

Appendix A: Pre-school Enrollment with Alternative Definitions

Given changes in the structure and starting ages of pre-school and primary school education in Brazil during the period explored (1996–2009), there are several possible ways to compute pre-school enrollment rates. Except where otherwise indicated, we always compute the share of children aged 4–6 that are enrolled in institutions intended for children in that age group. Before 2007, this is pre-school; beginning in 2007, this is either pre-school or primary schools because starting in 2007, six-year-olds were (gradually) included in Year 1 of Primary and Lower Secondary. Table A.1 compares our pre-school enrollment rate in each year during 1996–2009 with the share of 4–6 year-olds in school (whether in pre-school or primary school). This measure equals our measure in 2007 and later. Prior to 2007, the measures differ due to children ages 4–6 being enrolled in schools intended for older students. Table A.1 also shows the share of 4–5 year-olds in school in each year (an age group for which pre-school is always the intended level of education).

Table A.1: ECE enrollment rate by year and definition of enrollment

Year	Pre-school enrollment rate (% share of age 4–6 population enrolled in institutions intended for children that age)	Share of age 4–6 population enrolled in any school (%)	Share of age 4–5 population enrolled in any school (%)
1996	48	54	43
1997	51	56	47
1998	51	58	47
1999	52	60	50
2001	57	66	55
2002	58	67	57
2003	60	68	59
2004	61	71	61
2005	63	72	63
2006	65	76	68
2007	78	78	70
2008	80	80	73
2009	81	81	75

Source: MEC.

Appendix B: Survey of Evidence for Early Child Education in Brazil

In Brazil, the evidence on early child education is expanding. Table B.1 presents a collection of studies examining the issue.

Table B.1: Survey of studies of impact of ECE in Brazil

Study	Location & Data	Design	Results
Barros et al. (2011a)	Rio de Janeiro Child development test, observational instrument 2001	Multivariate regression	Impact of *high quality* creche • Higher quality creches across various dimensions led to better cognitive, social, and physical development
Barros et al. (2011b)	Rio de Janeiro Administrative data, questionnaire	Randomized assignment	Impact of creche • Double labor force participation of initially out-of-work mothers
Felício, Menezes and Zoghbi (2010)	Sertãozinho (São Paulo) Provinha Brasil, student questionnaire	Multivariate regression, propensity score matching	Impact of ECE • Students who entered school at 3, 4, or 5 had 6% higher literacy in 2nd grade
Fundação Carlos Chagas (2010)	Six state capitals Provinha Brasil, ECERS-R	Multivariate regression	Impact of *high quality* pre-school • Significant impact of higher quality pre-school on Portuguese test score in 2nd grade
Pazello and Almeida (2010)	National SAEB, PNAD (1993–2007)	Multivariate regression	Impact of pre-school • No significant impact on primary school completion
Rodrigues, Pinto and Santos (2010)	National SAEB, Unified Health System (SUS)	Instrumental variables	Impact of creche • Improvement in math test scores in 4th grade of 0.1 standard deviations
Calderini and Souza (2009)	National Prova Brasil 2005	Instrumental variables	Impact of pre-school • Improvement in math and Portuguese test scores in 4th grade
Curi and Menezes-Filho (2009)	National PPV & SAEB	Multivariate regression cross-sectional analysis	Impact of pre-school • Increased primary, lower secondary, secondary, and college completion • Increased standardized test scores in 4th, 8th, and 11th grades • Increased total years of schooling and wages • Impact of creche • Increased secondary and college completion
Natenzon (2003)	National SAEB, PNAD (1993–2001)	Multivariate regression	Impact of pre-school • No impact on math or Portuguese test scores in 4th grade
Felício and Vasconcellos (2007)	National SAEB 2003, Prova Brasil 2005	Propensity score matching, fixed effects	Impact of ECE • Students from ECE had higher math scores in 4th grade
Young (2001)	SE & NE regions Pesquisa sobre Padrões de Vida (PPV) 1997	Multivariate regression cross-sectional analysis	Impact of pre-school • Increased years of education (particularly for low-income children) • Reduced grade repetition • Improved earnings (for men)

Source: Authors.

Appendix C: Rio de Janeiro's Creche Lottery

Any child could register for the lottery for a given creche, after which households were split into three groups: Most Vulnerable, Middle Vulnerable, and Least Vulnerable (see figure C.1). A lottery was then held for one third of the creche vacancies among only the most vulnerable households. Children who won that lottery received spots in the creche. A second lottery was held for the next third of creche vacancies among the Middle Vulnerable children and the Most Vulnerable children who had lost the first lottery (i.e., they had a second chance to enter). Finally, a third lottery was held for the final third of creche vacancies, among the Least Vulnerable children, as well as the Most Vulnerable and Middle Vulnerable who had lost the previous lotteries. In this way, *any child* had the possibility of receiving a creche vacancy, but the Most Vulnerable children had three different chances to win, whereas the Least Vulnerable children had only one.

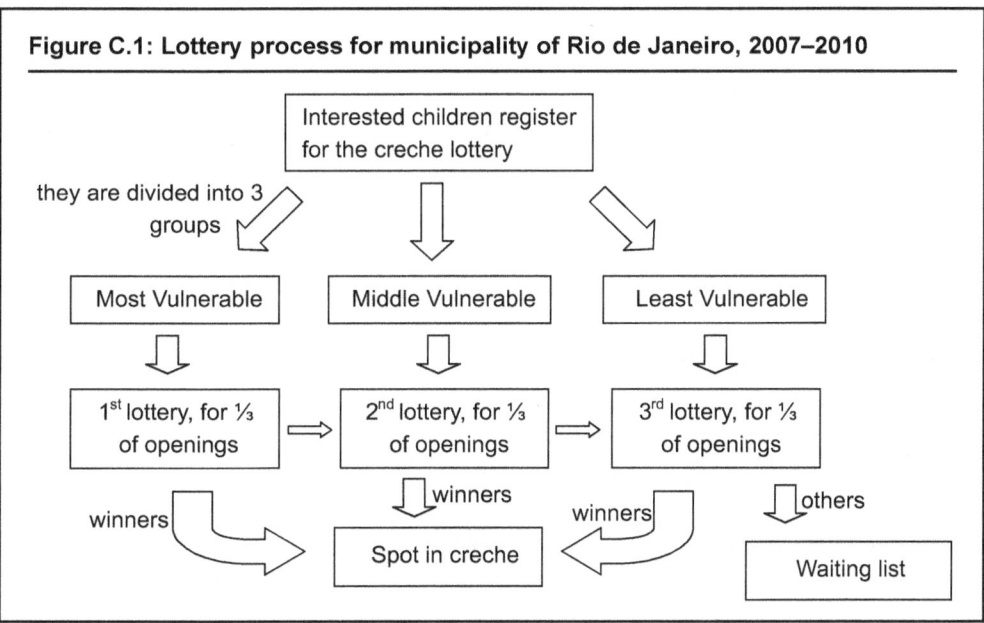

Figure C.1: Lottery process for municipality of Rio de Janeiro, 2007–2010

Source: Compiled by authors based on Barros et al. (2010).

Appendix D: Quality Rating Systems

Quality rating systems for Early Child Education in the United States generally evaluate the standards outlined in table D.1.

Table D.1: Quality standards used to rate ECD centers

Licensing Compliance	Family Partnerships
Ratio and Group Size	Administration and Management
Health and Safety	Cultural and Linguistic Diversity
Curriculum	Accreditation
Environment	Provisions for Special Needs
Child Assessment	Community Involvement
Staff Qualifications	

Source: Adapted from Tout et al. (2010).
Note: Each QRS employs only a subset of these standards.

The programs all use a building blocks rating structure, a points rating structure, or some combination of the two, then assigning the programs a number of stars as a quality rating. For example, the Oklahoma QRS employs a building blocks system: centers must satisfy minimum licensing requirements to achieve Level 1, possess weekly lesson plans, a daily reading program, and other factors, to reach Level 2, and so on (see table D.2 for details). Without satisfying all of the requirements for Level 2, a center cannot progress to Level 3. On the other hand, the Colorado system employs points: ECD centers may choose from a range of factors that improve the learning environment such as staff training and child-staff ratio, earning points for each factor and then achieving different levels for points earned.

Table D.2: Rating systems for early child development centers

Level	Requirements	Components rated
Oklahoma's Reaching for the Stars system—block-based system		
1	1 star is automatic with license	Minimum licensing requirements
2	Apply and meet criteria	Above plus teacher and director training, weekly lesson plans, activity interest areas, daily reading program, parent involvement (Centers must proceed to Level 3 within two years or they revert to Level 1)
3	Apply and meet criteria *or* national accreditation	Above plus teacher credentials, salary compensation, program evaluation including Environmental Rating Scales (ERSs)
4	Apply and meet criteria *and* national accreditation	Same as above
Colorado's (United States) Qualistar Early Learning system—point-based system		
0	0–9 points	Learning environment; family partnership; staff training and education; group size and child-staff ratio; accreditation
1	10–17 points	Same as above
2	18–25 points	Same as above
3	26–33 points	Same as above
4	34–42 points	Same as above

Source: Adapted from Zellman and Perlman (2008), tables 3.1 and 3.2.

Appendix E: Selected Child Development Instruments

Table E.1 presents a list of some of the instruments used in measuring child cognitive and social development in creches and pre-schools. A more complete list can be found in Fernald et al. (2009).

Table E.1: Sample of child assessment instruments used in creches and pre-schools

Instrument	Screening tool vs. assessment of abilities	Ratings & reports vs. direct assessment
Ages & Stages	Screening	Ratings & reports
Ages & Stages—Socio-emotional	Screening	Ratings & reports
Parents' Evaluation of Developmental Status	Screening	Ratings & reports
Brief Infant Toddler Social Emotional Assessment	Screening	Ratings & reports
Ounce Scale	Assessment of abilities	Ratings & reports
Pre-school and Kindergarten Behavior Scales	Both	Ratings & reports
High/Scope Child Observation Record for Infants and Toddlers	Assessment of abilities	Ratings & reports

Source: Fernald et al. (2009).

Appendix F: Curriculum for Primeira Infância Completa

Table F.1 shows the curriculum implemented as of November 2009.

Table F.1: Curriculum implemented as of November 2009

Week	Topic	Responsible secretariat
1	Within the PIC	Education/Health/Social Assistance
2	Health at the childcare center	Health
3	Baby on the development path	Education
4	And the family, how is it?	Social Assistance
5	Good treatment: Your child deserves it	Health
6	In my time, children were like this	Education
7	Family planning	Health
8	Present parent!	Social Assistance
9	Congratulations: Child Development	Education
10	Growing and developing healthily	Health
11	Food, fun, and art	Health
12	I want to see you smile	Health
13	Affectionate habits	Education
14	Diarrhea: When there is a risk of dehydration	Health
15	Dedicating time to your child	Education
16	Being a child isn't easy	Education
17	Who tells a story?	Education
18	Pirlimpimpim: The world of make believe	Education
19	Getting current on vaccinations	Health
20	Illnesses that color and mark	Health
21	Affection: Beyond words and gestures	Education
22	Limits: Yes, yes, no, no	Education
23	Mental health	Health
24	Breathe Rio without allergies	Health
25	The environment = my environment	Education
26	Rights of the child	Social assistance
27	Games are a serious thing	Education
28	Prevention of accidents	Health
29	Domestic violence	Social assistance
30	Community councils	Social assistance
31	Unified Health System	Health
32	The essence of childhood	Education
33	Diversity	Education
34	Children and the media	Education
35	Leisure for all	Education
36	Gender issues	Education
37	Sexuality in early childhood	Social assistance/Health
38	Strategy for family health	Health
39	Family and community living	Social assistance
40	The importance of civil registration	Social assistance

Source: Secretariat of Education, Municipality of Rio de Janeiro.

Appendix G: Selection of MEC Publications for Early Childhood Development

Table G.1 shows a selection of MEC publications for ECE. A full list of available MEC publications for ECE is available at the website of the Secretary for Basic Education in the Ministry of Education (MEC n.d.).

Table G.1: Selection of MEC publications for ECE

Publication title	Date
Orientações sobre convênios entre secretarias municipais de educação e instituições comunitárias, confessionais ou filantrópicas sem fins lucrativos para a oferta de educação infantil	2009
Indicadores da Qualidade na Educação Infantil	2009
Critérios para um Atendimento em Creches que Respeite os Direitos Fundamentais das Crianças, 2ª. ed.	2009
Educação Infantil: Saberes e práticas da inclusão	2006
Parâmetros Nacionais de Qualidade para a Educação Infantil	2006
Política Nacional de Educação Infantil	2006
Parâmetros Básicos de Infra-estrutura para Instituições de Educação Infantil	2006
Referencial curricular nacional para a educação infantil	1998

Source: MEC.

Appendix H: Jamaica's National Strategic Plan for Early Childhood Development

Table H.1 outlines Jamaica's National Strategic Plan for ECE.

Table H.1: Jamaica's National Strategic Plan for Early Childhood Development

Processes to improve early child development	Sample associated activity
Effective parenting education and support	Ensure that antenatal, child health clinics and ECIs provide parenting advice, education, and support for parents
Effective preventive health care	Develop a certification system to ensure that child health clinics provide the highest quality services
Early and effective screening, diagnosis and intervention for "at risk" children and households	Develop and put in place a national policy on screening and early identification for children and households that are "at risk"
Safe, learner-centered, well-maintained early childhood institutions facilities	Inspect ECIs regularly to ensure they maintain high standards
Effective curriculum delivery by trained ECD Practitioners	Provide all ECIs with an approved early childhood curriculum
Working environment processes	
All the persons and organizations who work with children or provide programs and services for them must work together to achieve the targets set	Put laws in place to govern the early childhood sector
Decisions on how to improve the quality of early childhood development in Jamaica must be made based on timely, clear, current, and accurate information	Put in place a computerized system to collect, store and manage important information about young children and their families

Source: Early Childhood Comission (2009).

References

Almond, Douglas, and Janet Currie. "Human capital development before age five." *Handbook of Labor Economics*, 2011, 1315–1486.

Armecin, Graeme, Jere Behrman, Paulita Duazo, Sharon Ghuman, Socorro Gultiano, Elizabeth King, and Nannette Lee. *Early Childhood Development through Integrated Programs: Evidence from the Philippines*. Policy Research Working Paper 3922, Washington, DC: World Bank, 2006.

Arnett, J. "Caregivers in Day-care Centers: Does Training Matter?" *Journal of Applied Developmental Psychology*, 1989: 541–552.

Aud, Susan, Michael Planty, Thomas Snyder, Kevin Bianco, Mary Ann Fox, Lauren Frohlich, Jana Kemp, and Lauren Drake. *The Condition of Education 2010*. NCES 2010–028, Washington DC: National Center for Education Statistics, Institute of Education Sciences, U.S. Department of Education, 2010.

Baker, Michael, Jonathan Gruber, and Kevin Milligan. "Universal Childcare, Maternal Labor Supply, and Family Well-Being." *Journal of Political Economy*, 2008.

Barnard, Wendy, Wendy Etheridge Smith, Richard Fiene, and Kelly Swanson. *Evaluation of Pennsylvania's Keystone STARS Quality Rating System in Child Care Settings*. Pittsburgh, PA: University of Pittsburgh Office of Child Development, 2006.

Barnett, W. Steven. "Better Teachers, Better Preschools: Student Achievement Linked to Teacher Qualifications." *Preschool Policy Matters* (NIEER), 2003.

———. "Benefits of Preschool Education" (presentation), 2004. www.nieer.org/resources/files/BarnettBenefits.ppt (accessed May 3, 2012).

Barnett, W. Steven, J Tarr, C Lamy, and E Frede. *Children's Educational Needs and Community Capacity in the Abbott Districts*. New Brunswick, NJ: Center for Early Education, Rutgers University, 1999.

———. *Fragile Lives, Shattered Dreams: A Report on Implementation of Preschool Education in New Jersey's Abbott Districts*. New Brunswick, NJ: National Institute for Early Education Research, Rutgers University, 2001.

Barnett, W. Steven, K Brown, and R Shore. "The Universal vs. Targeted Debate: Should the United States Have Preschool for All?" *Preschool Policy Matters 6*, 2004.

Barros, Ricardo Paes, Mirela Carvalho, Samuel Franco, Eduardo Pádua, and Andrezza Rosalém. "The Experience of the Municipality of Rio de Janeiro in Providing Day Care Services for Children Aged 0 to 3." Background paper for World Bank Brazil ECD study, Rio de Janeiro, 2010.

Barros, Ricardo Paes, Mirela Carvalho, Samuel Franco, Rosane Mendonça, and Andrezza Rosalém. "A Short-Term Cost-Effectiveness Evaluation of Better Quality Daycare Centers." Inter-American Development Bank Working Paper 239, 2011a.

Barros, Ricardo Paes, Mirela Carvalho, Samuel Franco, Andrezza Rosalém, and Daniel Santos. *Componentes para um sistema de monitoramento utilizando o ASQ3*. Powerpoint presentation given on February 25, 2011, at the Ministry of Planning in Santiago, Chile, Rio de Janeiro: IPEA, 2011b.

Barros, Ricardo Paes, Pedro Olinto, Trine Lunde, and Mirela Carvalho. *The Impact of Free Childcare on Women's Labor Force Participation: Evidence from Low-Income Neighborhoods of Rio de Janeiro.* Conference Paper, World Bank Economists' Forum, 2011c.

Bedard, Kelly, and Elizabeth Dhuey. "The Persistence of Early Childhood Maturity: International Evidence of Long-Run Age Effects." *Quarterly Journal of Economics*, 2006.

Bennett, John. *Benchmarks for Early Childhood Services in OECD Countries.* Innocenti Working Paper 2008–02, Florence: UNICEF Innocenti Research Centre, 2008.

———. "Early Childhood Education and Care Systems in the OECD Countries: The Issue of Tradition and Governance." *Encyclopedia on Early Childhood Development.* July 8, 2008. http://www.child-encyclopedia.com/documents/BennettANGxp.pdf (accessed February 15, 2011).

Berk, L. "Relationship of Caregiver Education to Child-Oriented Attitudes, Job Satisfaction, and Behaviors toward Children." *Child Care Quarterly*, 1985: 103–109.

Berlinski, S, S Galiani, and Paul Gertler. "The Effect of Pre-Primary Education on Primary School Performance." *Journal of Public Economics*, 2009: 219–234.

Black, S, P Devereux, and K Salvanes. "Too Young to Leave the Nest? The Effects of School Starting Age." *NBER Working Paper 13969*, 2008.

Blau, DM. "The Production of Quality in Child Care Centers: Another Look." *Applied Developmental Science*, 2000: 136–148.

Bobonis, Gustavo J, Edward Miguel, and Charu Puri-Sharma. "Anemia and School Participation." *Journal of Human Resources*, 2006.

Boulding, Carew, and Brian Wampler. "Voices, Votes, and Resources: Evaluating the Effect of Participatory Democracy on Well-being." *World Development*, 2010: 125–135.

Boyd, Brenda J, and Mary R Wandschneider. *Washington State Child Care Career and Wage Ladder Pilot Project.* Phase 2 Final Evaluation Report, Pullman, WA: Department of Human Development, Washington State University, 2004.

Browne, Gina, Carolyn Byrne, Jacqueline Roberts, Amiram Gafni, and Susan Whittaker. "When the Bough Breaks: Provider-Initiated Comprehensive Care Is More Effective and Less Expensive for Sole-Support Parents on Social Assistance." *Social Science & Medicine*, 2001: 1697–1710.

Bruder, Mary Beth, Cristina Mogro-Wilson, Vicki D Stayton, and Sylvia L Dietrich. "The National Status of In-Service Professional Development Systems for Early Intervention and Early Childhood Special Education Practitioners." *Infants & Young Children*, 2009: 13–20.

Bruns, Barbara, Andrea Tokman, Amy Walter, and Carla Cutolo. *Institutional Framework for Early Childhood Development in Chile.* Policy Note, Washington, DC: World Bank, 2010.

Calderini, SR, and AP Souza. "Pré-escola no Brasil: Seu Impacto na Qualidade da Educação Fundamental." *Anais do XXXVII Encontro da Anpec.* Foz do Iguaçu, Paraná, 2009. 1–21.

Campos, Maria Malta, Jodette Fullgraf, and Verena Wiggers. "Brazilian Early Childhood Education Quality: Some Research Results." *Cadernos de Pesquisa*, 2006: 87–128.

Carvalho, Mirela, and others. "Validating a Brazilian version of the ASQ-3." Draft report, 2011.

City University of New York. *The Educational Incentive Program (EIP)*. http://www.early-childhoodnyc.org/education/EIP.cfm (accessed February 9, 2011).

Cochran, Moncrieff. "International Perspectives on Early Childhood Education." *Educational Policy*, 2011: 65–91.

Cryer, Debby, Wolfgang Tietze, and Holger Wessels. "Parents' Perceptions of Their Children's Child Care: A Cross-National Comparison." *Early Childhood Research Quarterly*, 2002: 259–277.

Cryer, Debby, and Margaret Burchinal. "Parents as Child Care Consumers." *Early Childhood Research Quarterly*, 1997: 35–58.

Curi, AZ, and NA Menezes-Filho. "A relação entre educação pré-primária, salários, escolaridade e proficiência escolar no Brasil." *Estudos Econômicos (São Paulo)*, 2009: 39(4).

Department of Education & Early Childhood Development. *Scholarships and Incentives.* September 21, 2010. http://www.education.vic.gov.au/careers/earlychildhood/scholarships/default.htm (accessed February 9, 2011).

Dunn, LS. "Proximal and distal features of day care quality and children's development." *Early Childhood Research Quarterly*, 1993: 167–192.

Early Childhood Commission. *A Reader Friendly Guide to The National Strategic Plan for Early Childhood Development in Jamaica: 2008–2013*. Kingston: The Early Childhood Commission, 2009.

Early, Diane, Donna Bryant, Robert Pianta, Richard Clifford, Margaret Burchinal, Sharon Ritchie, Carollee Howes, and Oscar Barbarin. "Are teachers' education, major, and credentials related to classroom quality and children's academic gains in pre-kindergarten?" *Early Childhood Research Quarterly*, 2006: 174–195.

Early, Diane, Kelly Maxwell, Margaret Burchinal, Soumya Alva, Randall Bender, Donna Bryant, Karen Cai, Richard Clifford, Caroline Ebanks, James Griffin, Gary Henry, Carollee Howes, Jeniffer Iriondo-Perez, Hyun-Joo Jeon, Andrew Mashburn, Ellen Peisner-Feinberg, Robert Pianta, Nathan Vandergrift, and Nicholas Zill. "Teachers' Education, Classroom Quality, and Young Children's Academic Skills: Results From Seven Studies of Preschool Programs." *Child Development* 78, no. 2 (2007): 558–580.

Engle, Patrice, Maureen Black, Jere Behrman, Meena Cabral de Melo, Paul Gertler, Lydia Kapiriri, Reynaldo Martorell, Mary Eming Young, and the International Child Development Steering Group. "Strategies to avoid the loss of developmental potential in more than 200 million children in the developing world." *Lancet*, 2007: 229–242.

European Council Conclusions. "Barcelona European Council 15 and 16 March 2002." SN 100/1/02/02 http://www.consilium.europa.eu/ueDocs/cms_Data/docs/pressData/en/ec/71025.pdf, Barcelona, 2002.

Eurydice. "Compulsory Education in Europe 2010/2011." http://eacea.ec.europa.eu/education/eurydice/documents/compulsory_education/106EN.pdf (accessed January 1, 2011).

Evans, David, and Katrina Kosec. *Access to Early Child Education in Brazil*. Background Paper, Washington DC: World Bank, 2011.

Felício, F, and L Vasconcellos. "O Efeito da Educação Infantil sobre o Desempenho Escolar Medido em Exames Padronizados." *Anais do XXXV Encontro da Anpec*. Recife, Pernambuco, 2007. 1–22.

Felício, F, RT Menezes, and AC Zoghbi. "The effects of early child education on literacy scores using data from a new Brazilian assessment tool." Working Paper, 2010.

Fernald, Lia, Patricia Kariger, Patrice Engle, and Abbie Raikes. *Examining Early Child Development in Low-Income Countries: A Toolkit for the Assessment of Children in the First Five Years of Life*. Washington DC: The World Bank, 2009.

FPG Child Development Institute. *Environment Rating Scales: Assessment Instruments for early childhood and child care program quality*. http://ers.fpg.unc.edu/ (accessed February 12, 2011).

Fundação Carlos Chagas. *Educação Infantil no Brasil: Avaliação Qualitativa e Quantitativa*. Final Report, Inter-American Development Bank, 2010.

Gibbs, Robyn, and Jenny Poskitt. *Report on the Evaluation of the Early Childhood Centres of Innovation Programme*. Evaluation Associates Ltd, 2009.

Gomes, JB. "Política Nacional de Educação Infantil No Brasil: Uma Luta Contínua, Uma Política Descontínua." 10.

Gormley, William, Jr, and Ted Gayer. "Promoting school readiness in Oklahoma: An evaluation of Tulsa's pre-k program." *The Journal of Human Resources*, 2006: 533–558.

Governo da Bahia. *Creche Nossa Senhora das Graças*. 2011. http://www.pm.ba.gov.br/creche2011/ (accessed February 23, 2011).

Grantham-McGregor, SM, SP Walker, SM Chang, and Powell CA. "Effects of early childhood supplementation with and without stimulation on later development in stunted Jamaican children." *American Journal of Clinical Nutrition* 66, no. 2 (1997): 247–253.

Gupta, N, and M Simonsen. "Effects of Universal Child Care Participation on Pre-teen Skills and Risky Behaviours." *European Association of Labor Economists Working Paper*, 2010.

Hanushek, Eric A, and L Woessman. "The Role of Cognitive Skills in Economic Development." *Journal of Economic Literature*, 2008: 607–668.

Hanushek, Eric A, and Steven G Rivkin. "Generalizations about Using Value-Added Measures of Teacher Quality." *American Economic Review*, 2010: 267–271.

Hanushek, Eric A, and Steven G Rivkin. "How to Improve the Supply of High Quality Teachers." In *Brookings Papers on Education Policy 2004*, by Diane (ed.) Ravitch, 7–25. Washington DC: Brookings Institution Press, 2004.

Harbison, R, and EA Hanushek. *Educational Performance of the Poor: Lessons from Rural Brazil*. New York: Oxford University Press, 1992.

Harms, T, D Cryer, and RM Clifford. *Infant/Toddler Environment Rating Scale (Rev. Ed.)*. New York: Teachers College Press, 2006.

Harms, T, RM Clifford, and D Cryer. *Early Childhood Environment Rating Scale (Rev. Ed.)*. New York: Teachers College Press, 2005.

Haskins, Ron, and W. Steven Barnett. "Finally, Obama administration is putting Head Start to the Test." *Washington Post*, October 11, 2010.

Heckman, James J, and Dimitriy V Masterov. "The Productivity Argument for Investing in Young Children." *Applied Economic Perspectives and Policy* 29, no. 3 (2007): 446–493.

Heckman, James J, SH Moon, R Pinto, P Savelyev, and A Yavitz. "The rate of return to the High/Scope Perry Preschool Program." *Journal of Public Economics*, 2010: 114–128.

Helburn, SW (ed.). *Cost, quality and child outcomes in child care centers.* Technical report, Denver: University of Colorado at Denver, Department of Economics, Center for Research in Economic and Social Policy, 1995.

Honig, AS, and A Hirallal. "Which counts more for excellence in childcare staff-years in service, education level or ECE coursework?" *Early Child Development & Care*, 1998: 31–46.

Howes, C. "Can the age of entry into child care and the quality of child care predict adjustment in kindergarten?" *Developmental Psychology*, 1990: 292–303.

———. "Children's experiences in center-based child care as a function of teacher background and adult-child ratio." *Merrill-Palmer Quarterly*, 1997: 404–425.

———. "Reconceptualizing the early childhood work force." In *Cost, quality, and child outcomes in child care centers. Technical report.*, by SW Helburn, 159–170. Denver: Department of Economics, Center for Research in Economic and Social Policy, 1995.

Howes, C, DC Phillips, and M Whitebook. "Teacher characteristics and effective teaching in child care: Findings from the National Child Care Staffing Study." *Child & Youth Care Forum*, 1992: 399–414.

Howes, C, R Pianta, D Bryant, B Hamre, J Downer, and S Soliday-Hong. *Ensuring Effective Teaching in Early Childhood Education through Linked Professional Development Systems, Quality Rating Systems and State Competencies: The Role of Research in an Evidence-Driven System.* White paper, Arlington VA: National Center for Research in Early Childhood Education, 2008.

INEP. "Ensino infantil: perfil das famílias com crianças de zero a cinco anos que frequentam a escola." *Na Medida*, 2009: 1(4): 4–9.

JIS News. "Jamaica's Early Childhood Strategic Plan Gaining Global Recognition ." *Jamaica Information Service*, August 12, 2010: http://www.jis.gov.jm/news/100/24993?mode=redirect.

Johns, S. "Early childhood service development and intersectoral collaboration in rural Australia." *Australian Journal of Primary Health*, 2010: 40–46.

Kosec, Katrina. *Politics and Preschool: The Political Economy of Investment in Pre-Primary Education.* World Bank Policy Research Working Paper 5647. http://go.worldbank.org/H6GMC7AWH0, 2011.

La Paro, KM, RC Pianta, and M Stuhlman. "Classroom Assessment Scoring System™ (CLASS™): Findings from the pre-k year." *Elementary School Journal*, 2004: 409–426.

LoCasale-Crouch, J, et al. "Observed classroom quality profiles in state-funded prekindergarten programs and associations with teacher, program, and classroom characteristics." *Early Childhood Research Quarterly*, 2007: 3–17.

Look for the Stars. "List of Required Documents for 2-, 3-, and 4-STAR Status." *New Mexico Kids: Look for the STARS Library*. September 22, 2005. http://www.newmexicokids.org/#.pages.library.stars.index.htm (accessed February 13, 2011).

Marshall, NL, CL Creps, NR Burstein, FB Glantz, WW Robeson, and WS Barnett. *The cost and quality of full day, year-round early care and education in Massachusetts preschool classrooms.* Cambridge: Wellesley Center for Women and Abt Associates, 2001.

Mashburn, Andrew J, et al. "Measures of Classroom Quality in Prekindergarten and Children's Development of Academic, Language, and Social Skills." *Child Development,* 2008: 732–749.

Masse, LN, and WS Barnett. "A benefit-cost analysis of the Abecedarian Early Childhood Intervention." In *Cost effectiveness and education policy,* by HM Levin and McEwan PJ. 2002.

Matthews, Clark. *Benchmarking Policies and Interventions in Early Childhood Development: Case Studies from Australia, New Zealand, England and Sweden.* Background paper, Washington DC: World Bank, 2010.

MEC. *Educação Infantil, Secretaria de Educação Básica, Ministério de Educação.* http://portal.mec.gov.br/index.php?option=com_content&view=article&id=12579%3Aeducacao-infantil&Itemid=859 (accessed March 10, 2011).

———. *Orientações sobre convênios entre secretarias municipais de educação e instituições comunitárias, confessionais ou filantrópicas sem fins lucrativos para a oferta de educação infantil.* Brasilia: MEC, SEB, 2009.

———. *Orientações sobre convênios entre secretarias municipais de educação e instituições comunitárias, confessionais ou filantrópicas sem fins lucrativos para a oferta de educação infantil.* Brasilia: MEC, SEB, 2009.

———. *Programa Nacional Biblioteca da Escola | Ministério de Educação.* 2009. http://portal.mec.gov.br/index.php?option=com_content@view=article&id=12368@Itemid=574 (accessed February 15, 2011).

Melo, Marcus Andre. "Democratizing Budgeting Decisions and Execution in Brazil: More Participatation or Redesign of Formal Institutions?" In *Participatory Innovation and Representative Democracy in Latin America,* by Andrew Selee and Enrique Peruzzotti. Baltimore: The Johns Hopkins University Press, 2009.

Miguel, Edward, and Michael Kremer. "Worms: Identifying Impacts on Education and Health in the Presence of Treatment Externalities." *Econometrica,* 2004: 159–217.

MINED. "Subvención Escolar Preferencial." *Gobierno de Chile | Ministerio de Educación.* 2011. http://www.mineduc.cl/index.php?id_portal=29 (accessed March 5, 2011).

Ministério da Saúde do Brasil. *Bolsa Família na Saúde (MS-DATASUS).* http://bolsafamilia.datasus.gov.br/w3c/bfa_relconsol.asp (accessed February 7, 2011).

Ministério de Educação. *Política Nacional da Educação Infantil: pelo direito das crianças de zero a seis anos à Educação.* Secretaria de Educação Básica, Ministério de Educação, 2006.

Moço, Anderson. "Balanço do Plano Nacional de Educação (PNE) 2001–2010." *Nova Escola,* March 2010: http://revistaescola.abril.com.br/politicas-publicas/legislacao/pne-plano-nacional-de-educacao-537431.shtml.

Muralidharan, Karthik, and Venkatesh Sundararaman. *Teacher Performance Pay: Experimental Evidence from India.* Working Paper No. 15323, NBER, 2009.

Muzzi, Mariana. *UNICEF Good Practices in Integrating Birth Registration into Health Systems (2000–2009); Case Studies: Bangladesh, Brazil, the Gambia and Delhi, India.* Working Paper, New York: UNICEF, 2010.

NACCRRA. *Parents' Perceptions of Child Care in the United States—NACCRRA's National Parent Poll: November 2008.* National Association of Child Care Resource & Referral Agencies, 2009.

NAEHCY. "SUMMARY OF HEAD START PROVISIONS ON HOMELESSNESS AND FOSTER CARE." *National Association for the Education of Homeless Children and Youth.* January 2008. http://www.naehcy.org/dl/headstartsum.pdf (accessed March 4, 2011).

NAEYC. *Child-Teacher Ratio Chart.* National Association for the Education of Young Children, 2008.

Natenzon, PE. *Efeitos da Educação Pré-Escolar no Brasil.* Monograph, Departamento de Economia da Faculdade de Economia, Administração e Contabilidade da Universidade de São Paulo, 2003.

National Association for Regulatory Administration & National Child Care Information and Technical Assistance Center. "The 2005 Child Care Licensing Study." Final Report, 2006.

NGA. *Partnering with the Private and Philanthropic Sectors: A Governor's Guide to Investing in Early Childhood.* http://www.nga.org/Files/pdf/0806PARTNERINGEDUCATION.pdf, Washington, DC: National Governor's Assocation Center for Best Practices, 2008.

Nores, Milagros, and W. Steven Barnett. "Benefits of early childhood interventions across the world: (Under) Investing in the very young." *Economics of Education Review*, April 2010: 271–282.

OECD. *Starting Strong II: Early Childhood Education and Care.* Annex E, OECD Publishing, 2006.

OHS. "Head Start Program Fact Sheet, Fiscal Year 2010." *U.S. Department of Health & Human Services, Administration for Children & Families, Office of Head Start.* February 2010. http://www.acf.hhs.gov/programs/ohs/about/fy2010.html (accessed March 5, 2011).

Paiva, Maria da Graça Gomes, Alessandra Schneider, Maria Lúcia Salle Machado, and Pollyana Vilela Duarte Perinazzo. "A New Look on Early Child Care and Education (ECCE) as Joint Responsibility." *Current Issues in Comparative Education*, 2009: 33–41.

Paraguassu, Lisandra. "Precisamos investir em qualidade." *O Estado de São Paulo*, January 5, 2011.

Parks, Casey. "Program launched to improve early childhood education." *The Oregonian*, May 11, 2009.

Paxson, Christina, and Norbert Schady. "Cognitive development among young children in Ecuador: The roles of wealth, health, and parenting." *Journal of Human Resources* 42, no. 1 (2007).

Pazello, ET, and RB Almeida. "O efeito da pré-escola sobre o desempenho escolar futuro dos indivíduos." *ANPEC.* Salvador, 2010.

Primeira Infância Melhor. *PIM-Programa Primeira Infância Melhor-Noticiário.* February 3, 2011. http://www.pim.saude.rs.gov.br/a_PIM/php/pagina-Noticiario.php?n=63 (accessed February 25, 2011).

Rede Nacional Primeira Infância. "Plano Nacional pela Primeira Infância." 2010.

Rodrigues, CG, Christine XC Pinto, and Daniel D Santos. "The impact of daycare attendance on Math test scores for a cohort of 4th graders in Brazil." Working paper, 2010.

Ruopp, R, T Travers, F Glantz, and C Coelen. *Children at the Center: Final report of the National Day Care Study (vol 1)*. Cambridge: Abt Associates, 1979.

Ryan, Carey S, Robert McCall, Debbie Robinson, Christina Groark, Laurie Mulvey, and Bradford Plemons. "Benefits of the Comprehensive Child Development Program as a Function of AFDC Receipt and SES." *Child Development*, 2002: 315–328.

Sakai, LM, M Whitebook, A Wishard, and C Howes. "Evaluating the Early Childhood Environment Rating Scale (ECERS): Assessing Differences between the First and Revised Edition." *Early Childhood Research Quarterly* , 2003: 427–445.

Santarém. *Câmara de Santarém Lançou Programa Eco-Escolas*. June 14, 2010. http://www.cm-santarem.pt/pracapublica/noticias/Paginas/C%C3%A2maradeSantar%C3%A9mlan%C3%A7ouProgramaEco-Escolas.aspx (accessed February 15, 2011).

Saracho, ON, and B Spodek. "Early childhood teachers' preparation and the quality of program outcomes." *Early Child Development and Care*, 2007: 71–91.

Scarr, S, M Eisenberg, and K Deater-Deckard. "Measurement of quality in child care centers." *Early Childhood Research Quarterly*, 1994: 131–151.

Schneider, Alessandra, and Vera Regina Ramires. *Primeira Infância Melhor: uma inovação em política pública*. Brasilia: UNESCO, 2007.

Schneider, Alessandra, Vera Regina Ramires, Maria da Graça Gomes Paiva, and Leila Almeida. "The Better Early Childhood Development Program: An Innovative Brazilian Public Policy." *Current Issues in Comparative Education (Teachers College, Columbia University)*, 2009: 24–32.

Schweinhart, LJ, and DP Weikart. "Why curriculum matters in early childhood education." *Educational Leadership*, 1998: 57–60.

Schweinhart, LJ, HV Barnes, and DP Weikhart. "Significant Benefits: The High/Scope Perry Pre-school Study Through Age 27." In *Child Welfare: Major Themes in Health and Social Welfare*, by Nick Frost, 9–29. Abingdon, UK: Routledge, 2005.

Sharp, C. "School Starting Age: European Policy and Recent Research." 2002.

Shonkoff, Jack P, and Deborah Phillips. *From neurons to neighborhoods: the science of early child development*. Washington, DC: National Academy Press, 2000.

Silva, Maria do Pilar Lacerda Almeida. "Políticas Sociais para a primeira infância: Empreendedores Capeões em Investimento na Primeira Infância." *Brazilian Business Champions for Early Childhood Investment*. São Paulo, Brazil: Committee for Economic Development, 2010.

Silva, Verónica. *Chile Crece Contigo: Política Nacional de Desarrollo Infantil Temprano—Lecciones de política pública para la Primera Infancia*. PowerPoint Presentation, Washington DC: World Bank, 2010.

Snow, Catherine E, and Susan B (editors) Van Hemel. *Early Childhood Assessment: Why, What, and How*. Washington, DC: The National Academies Press, 2008.

Souza, Celina. "Participatory Budgeting in Brazilian Cities: Limits and Possibilities in Building Democratic Institutions." *Environment and Urbanization*, 2001: 159–184.

Springer, Matthew, Laura Hamilton, Daniel McCaffrey, Dale Ballou, Vi-Nhuan Le, Matthew Pepper, J.R. Lockwood, and Brian Stecher. *Teacher Pay for Performance: Experimental Evidence from the Project on Incentives in Teaching*. Nashville, TN: National Center for Performance Incentives at Vanderbilt University, 2010.

St. Pierre, Robert G, and Jean I Layzer. "Using Home Visits for Multiple Purposes: The Comprehensive Child Development Program." *The Future of Children*, 1999: 134–151.

Sylva, Kathy, Edward Melhuish, Pam Sammons, Siraj-Blatchford, and Brenda Taggart. *The Effective Provision of Pre-School Education (EPPE) Project*. Final Report, London: The Institute of Education, 2004.

Teachstone. *The Class Tool*. 2011. http://www.teachstone.org/about-the-class/ (accessed February 12, 2011).

Thornburg, Kathy R, Wayne A Mayfield, Jacqueline S Hawks, and Kathryn L Fuger. *The Missouri Quality Rating System School Readiness Study*. Columbia, MD: Center for Family Policy & Research, 2009.

Tietze, W, J Bairrão, TB Leal, and H Rossbach. "Assessing quality characteristics of center-based early childhood environments in Germany and Portugal: A cross-national study." *European Journal of Psychology of Education*, 1998: 283–298.

Tout, Kathryn, Rebecca Starr, Margaret Soli, Shannon Moodie, Gretchen Kirby, and Kimberly Boller. *The Child Care Quality Rating System (QRS) Assessment: Compendium of Quality Rating Systems and Evaluations*. Washington DC: Office of Planning, Research and Evaluation, Administration for Children and Families, Department of Health and Human Services, 2010.

Tribuna. "Asas da Florestania Infantil é sucesso." *A Tribuna: O Jornal de Todos os Acrianos*, December 15, 2010: http://www.jornaltribuna.com.br/MostrarNoticia.do?id=11828&ano=2010&mes=12&dia=15.

UNICEF. *Investimento Criança no Brasil de 2006 a 2009*. http://investimentocrianca.org.br/SimIC/InvestimentoCrianca.aspx (accessed February 5, 2011).

———. *Plano Nacional pela Primeira Infância será lançado no dia 7 de dezembro, em Brasília*. December 3, 2010. http://www.unicef.org/brazil/pt/media_19413.htm (accessed February 15, 2011).

Urzúa, Sergio, and Gregory Veramendi. "The Impact of Out-of-Home Childcare Centers on Early Childhood Development." Inter-American Development Bank Working Paper 240, 2011.

U.S. Department of Health & Human Services. "HHS Announces National Effort to Reshape and Raise Quality in Head Start Programs." *U.S. Department of Health & Human Services—HHS.gov*. September 21, 2010. http://www.hhs.gov/news/press/2010pres/09/20100921a.html (accessed February 8, 2011).

Vega, José Molinas, and Ricardo Paes de Barros. *Human Opportunities for Children in Brazil: An Assessment with the Human Opportunity Index*. Washington DC: World Bank, 2011.

Walker, Susan P, Susan M Chang, Christine A Powell, and Sally M Grantham-McGregor. "Effects of early childhood psychosocial stimulation and nutritional supplementation on cognition and education in growth-retarded Jamaican children: prospective cohort study." *Lancet*, 2005: Webappendix, 1–8.

Weber, Demétrio. "Ministro quer ensino médio em horário integral." *O Globo*, January 4, 2011.

Whitebook, Marcy. *Early Education Quality: Higher Teacher Qualifications for Better Living Environments—A Review of the Literature*. httP//eric.ed.gov/PDFS/ED481219.pdf, Center for the Study of Child Care Employment, Institute of Industrial Relations, University of California at Berkeley, 2003.

Whitebook, Marcy, and Laura Sakai. "Turnover begets turnover: an examination of job and occupational instability among child care center staff." *Early Childhood Research Quarterly*, 2003: 273–293.

Whitebook, Marcy, C Howes, and D Phillips. *The National Child Care Staffing Study. Final Report: Who cares? Child care teaches and the quality of care in America.* Washington DC: Center for the Child Care Workforce, 1990.

Whitebook, Marcy, L Sakai, E Gerber, and C Howes. *Then & now: Changes in child care staffing, 1994–2000.* Technical report., Washington DC: Center for the Child Care Workforce, 2001.

YMCA of Greater Seattle. *STARS Training.* 2011. http://www.seattlemca.org/page.cfm?id=youthSTARS (accessed February 9, 2011).

Yoshikawa, Hirokazu, Kathleen McCartney, Robert Myers, Kristen Bub, Julieta Lugo-Gil, Maria Ramos, Felicia Knaul. *Early Childhood Education in Mexico: Expansion, Quality Improvement, and Curricular Reform.* Innocenti Working Paper—IWP-2007-03, UNICEF, 2007.

Young, Mary Eming. *Brazil Early Child Development: A Focus on the Impact of Preschools.* No. 22841-BR, Washington, D.C.: World Bank, 2001.

Zellman, Gail L, and Michael Perlman. *Child-Care Quality Rating and Improvement Systems in Five Pioneer States.* Santa Monica, CA: RAND Corporation, 2008.

Zellman, Gail L, Michal Perlman, Vi-Nhuan Le, and Claude Messan Setodji. *Assessing the Validity of the Qualistar Early Learning Quality Rating and Improvement System as a Tool for Improving Child-Care Quality.* RAND report, Santa Monica, CA: RAND, 2008.

Zill, Nicholas, Gary Resnick, Kwang Kim, Ruth McKey, Cheryl Clark, Shefali Pai-Samant, David Connell, Michael Vaden-Kiernan, Robert O'Brien, Mary Ann D'Elio. *Head Start FACES: Longitudinal findings on program performance.* Third progress report, Washington DC: Research, Demonstration, and Evaluation Branch & Head Start Bureau, Administration on Children, Youth and Families, US Department of Health & Human Services, 2001.

ECO-AUDIT
Environmental Benefits Statement

The World Bank is committed to preserving endangered forests and natural resources. The Office of the Publisher has chosen to print World Bank Studies and Working Papers on recycled paper with 30 percent postconsumer fiber in accordance with the recommended standards for paper usage set by the Green Press Initiative, a nonprofit program supporting publishers in using fiber that is not sourced from endangered forests. For more information, visit www.greenpressinitiative.org.

In 2010, the printing of this book on recycled paper saved the following:
- 11 trees*
- 3 million Btu of total energy
- 1,045 lb. of net greenhouse gases
- 5,035 gal. of waste water
- 306 lb. of solid waste

* 40 feet in height and 6–8 inches in diameter

www.ingramcontent.com/pod-product-compliance
Lightning Source LLC
Chambersburg PA
CBHW081940170426
43202CB00018B/2959